RECORDED VERSIONS GUITAR

AUTHENTIC TRANSCRIPTIONS WITH NOTES AND TABLATURE

BLUES GUITAR TAB

T0071695

ISBN 978-1-4584-0531-9

HAL•LEONARD® CORPORATION

7777 W. BLUEMOUND RD. P.O. BOX 13819 MILWAUKEE, WI 53213

Visit Hal Leonard Online at
www.halleonard.com

Cookin'

By Duke Robillard

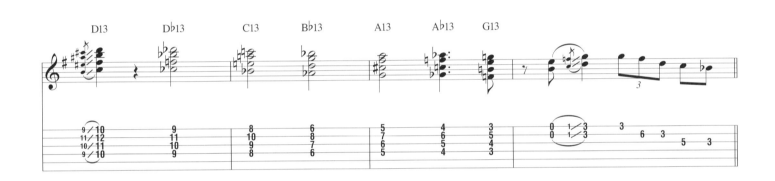

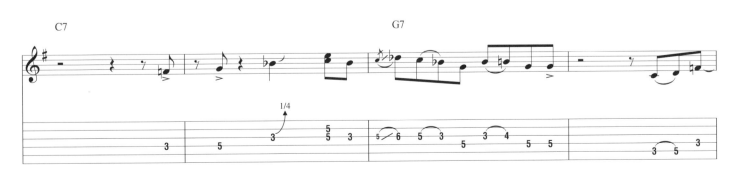

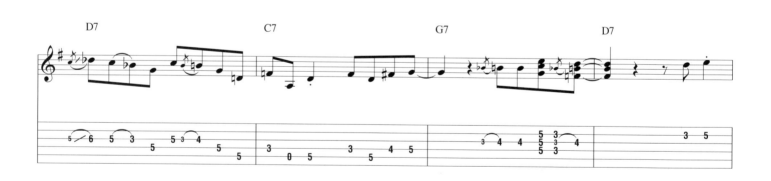

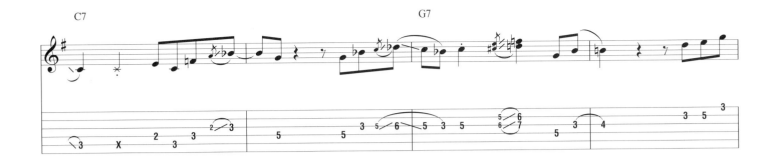

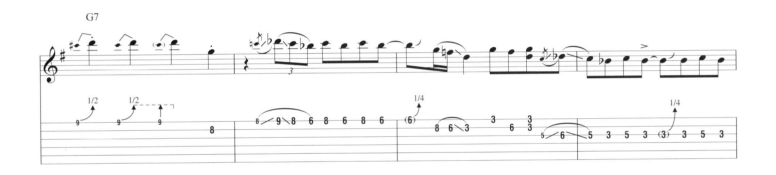

*3rd string sounded by pull off; don't pick.

rake ⌐

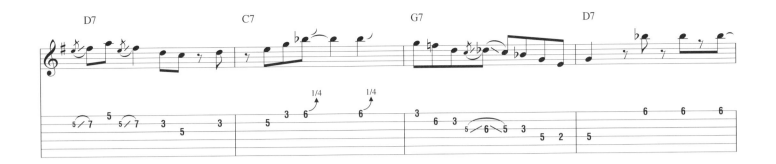

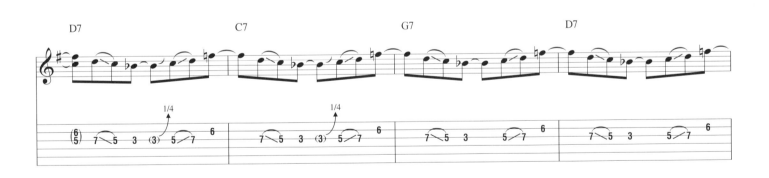

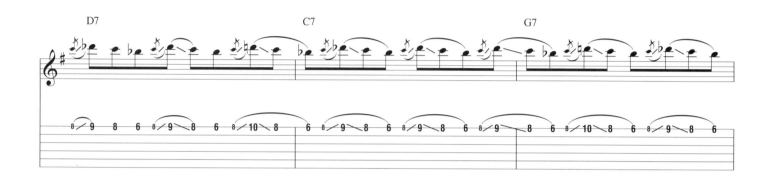

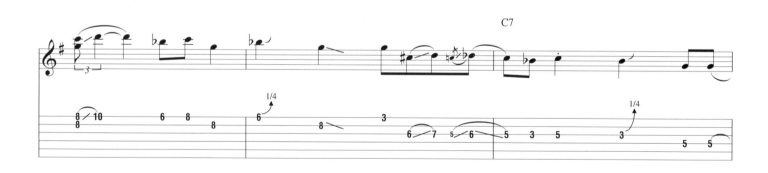

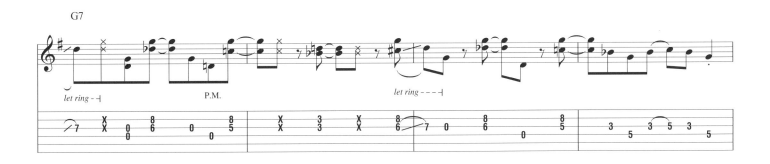

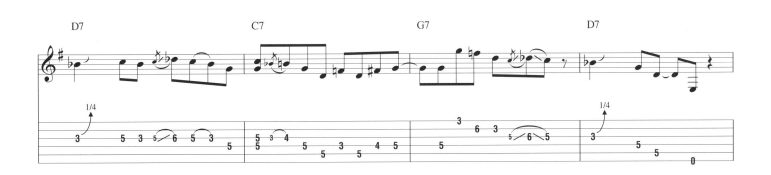

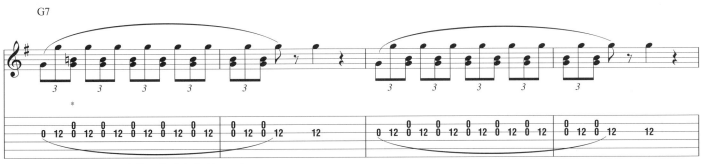

*2nd string sounded by pull-off; don't pick, next 4 meas.

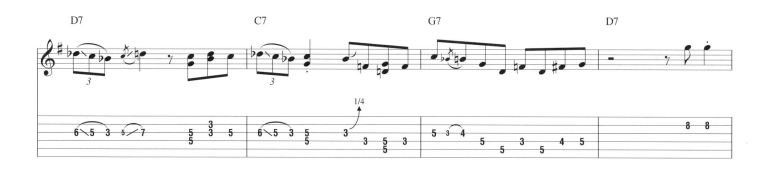

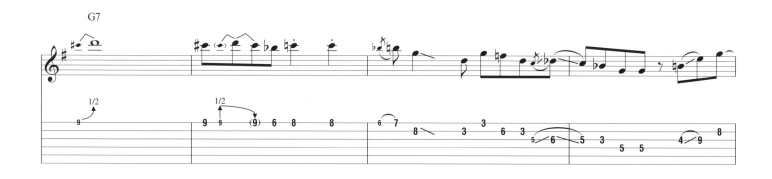

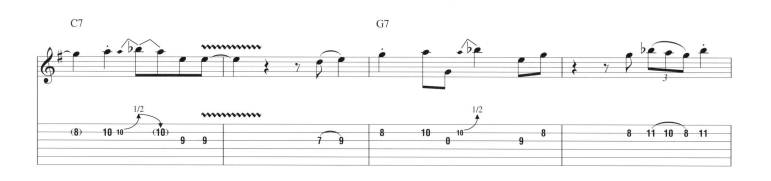

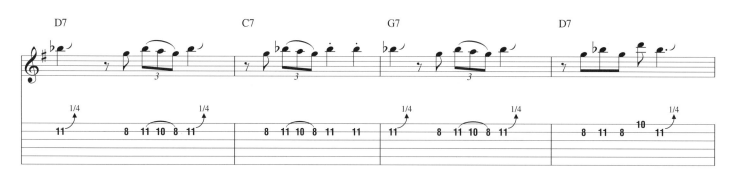

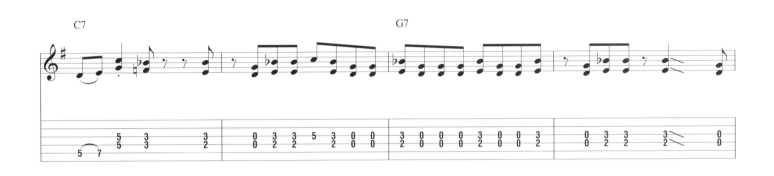

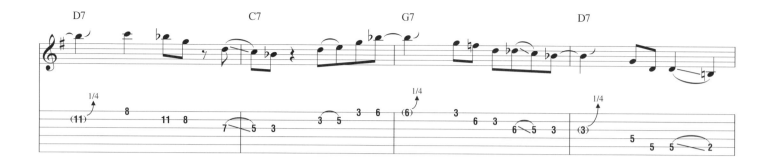

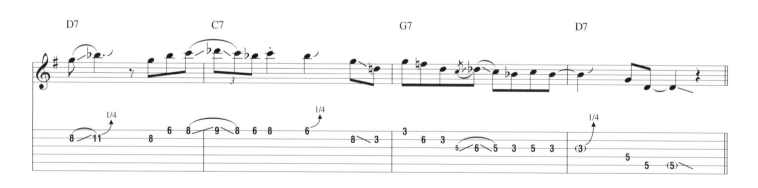

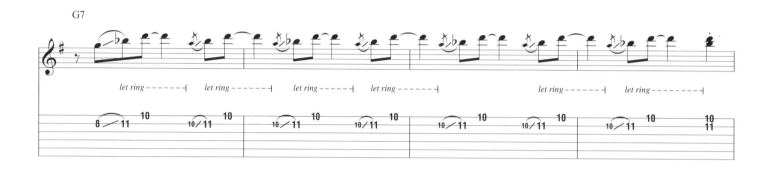

E

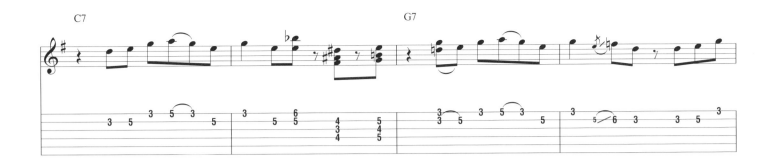

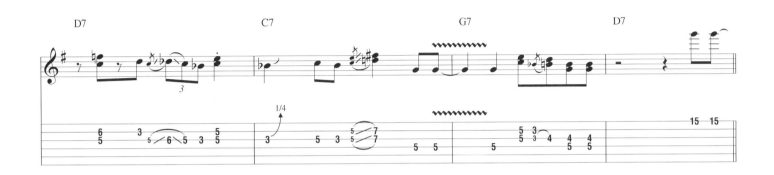

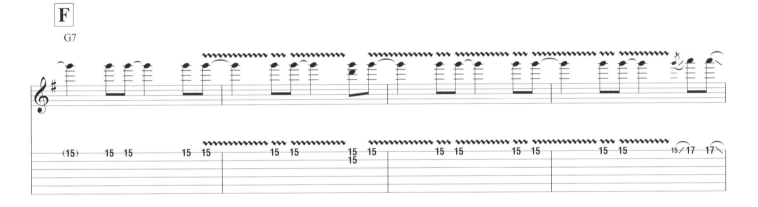

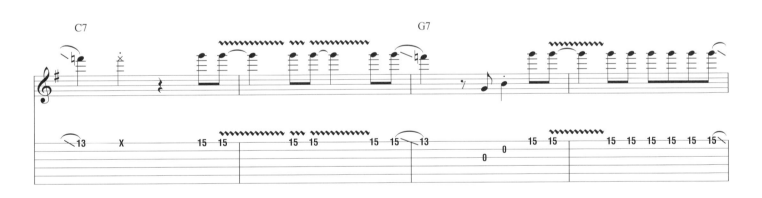

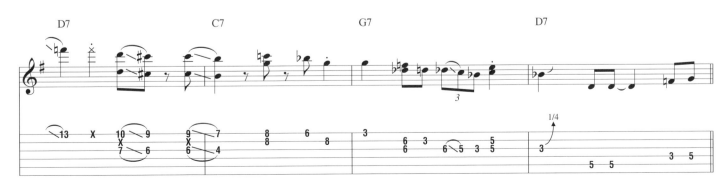

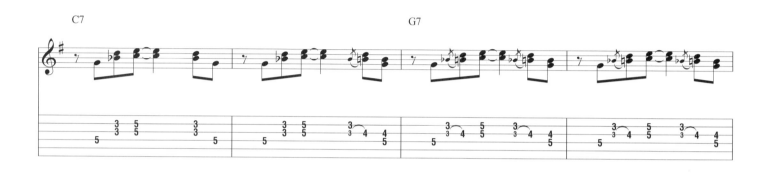

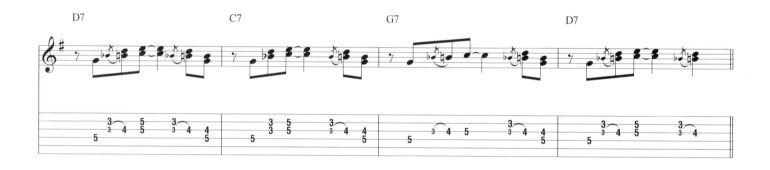

*T = Thumb on 6th string

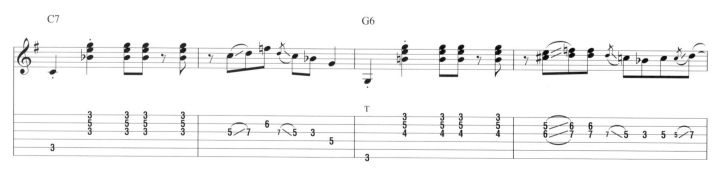

I

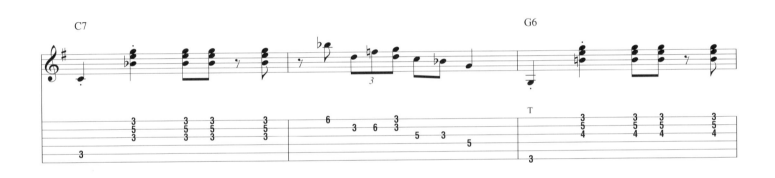

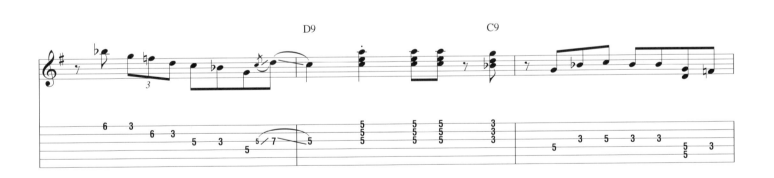

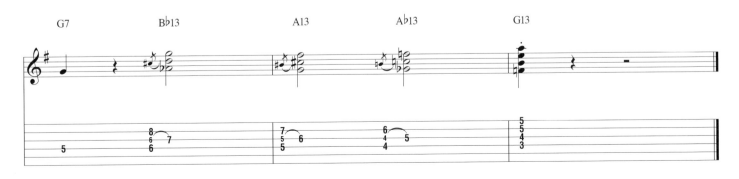

Cool Guitars

By Jeffrey Sutherland

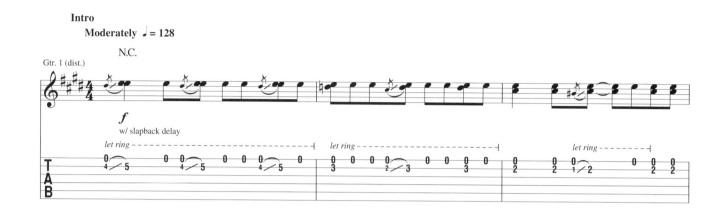

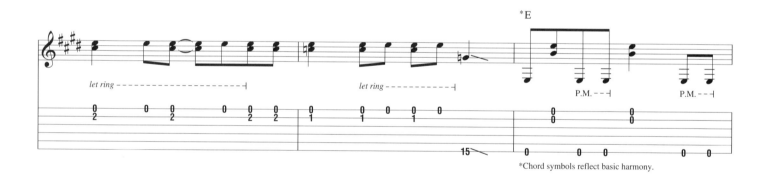

*Chord symbols reflect basic harmony.

my-self a cool guitar. 2. Well, she

Verse

nev-er should have called me a la-zy slob; it ain't com-plete-ly my fault I can't

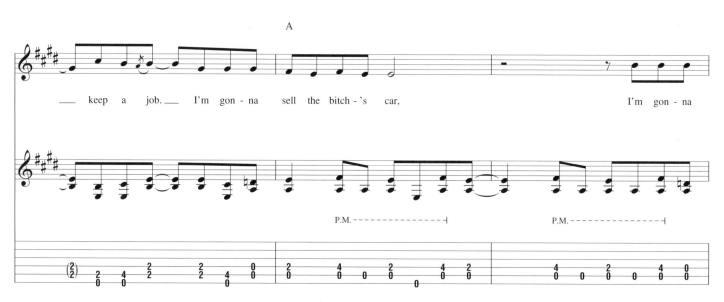

keep a job. I'm gon-na sell the bitch-'s car, I'm gon-na

Guitar Solo

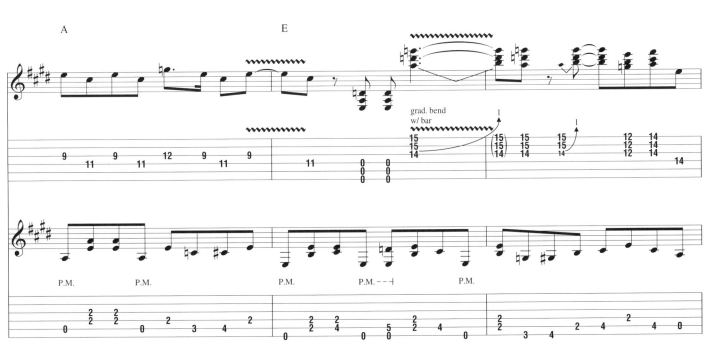

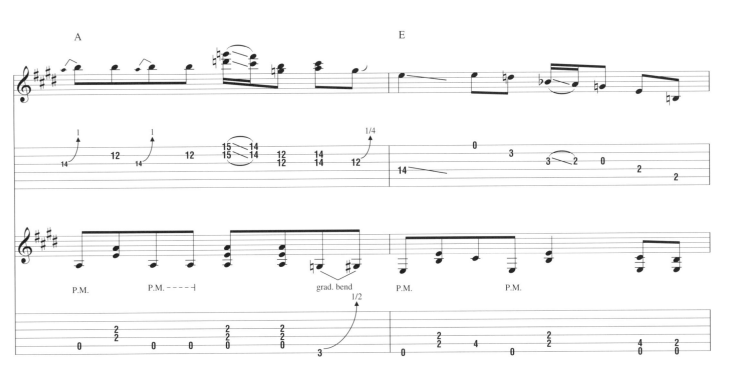

Interlude

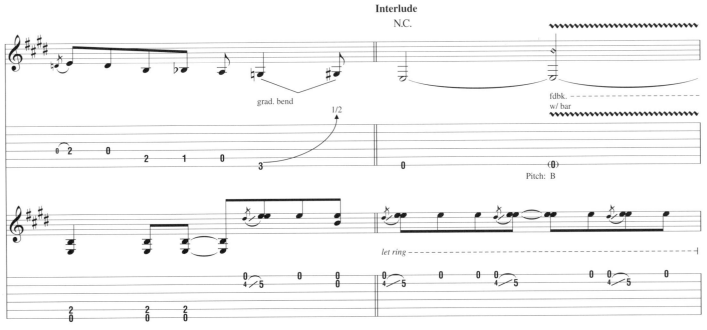

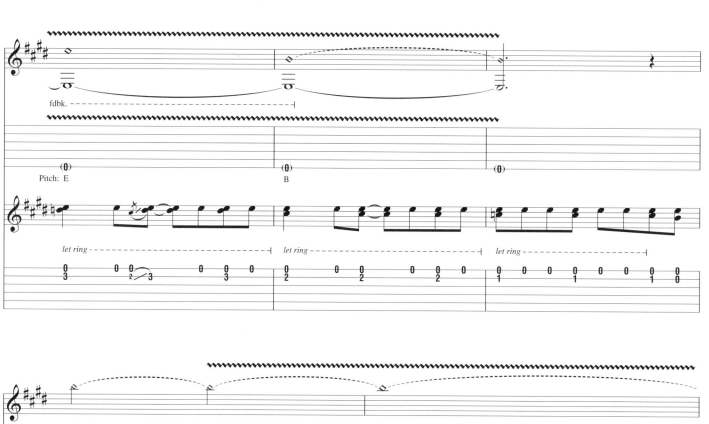

Pitch: E   B

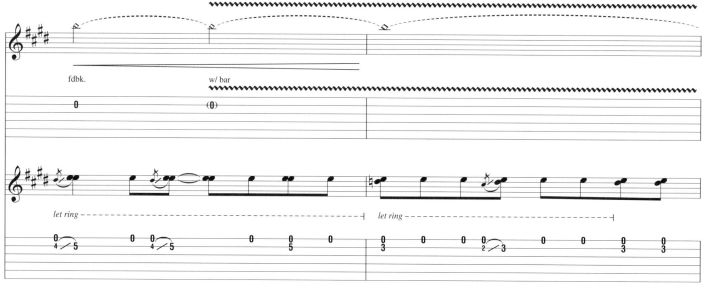

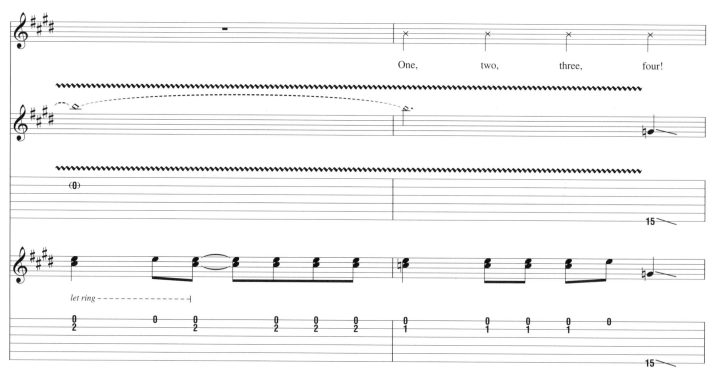

One,   two,   three,   four!

Verse

said I spent my mon-ey on te-qui-la and beer, ___ have-n't paid my fair share since this

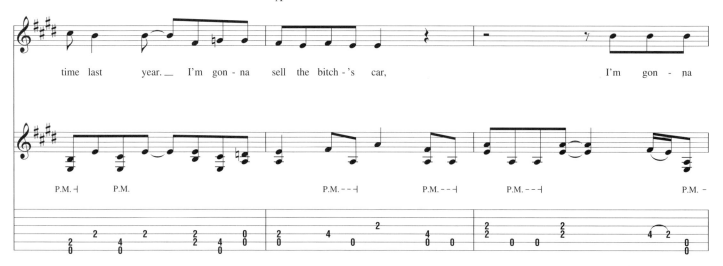

Verse

said she could-n't care less where I'll ___ spend my nights; ___ sor - ry thing 'bout it, she's

Free time

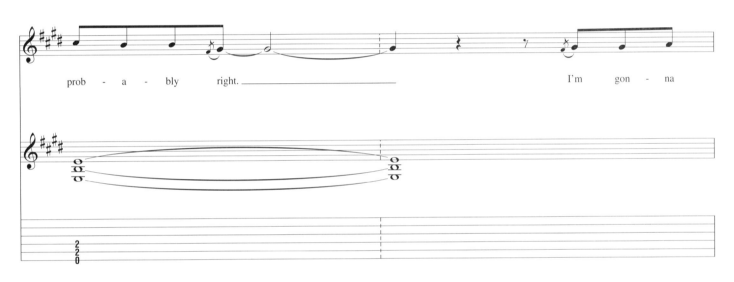

prob - a - bly right. _____ I'm gon - na

A tempo

sell the bitch -'s car, I'm gon - na sell the bitch -'s car.

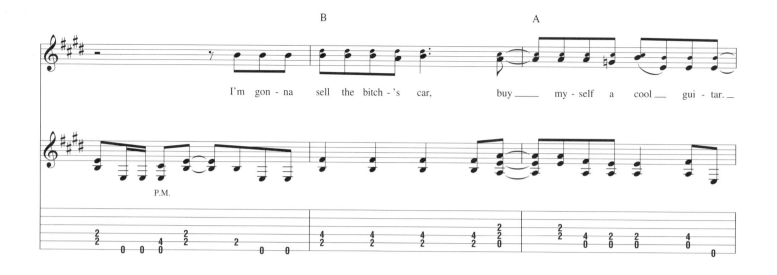

I'm gon-na sell the bitch-'s car, buy ___ my-self a cool ___ gui-tar. ___

I'm gon-na sell the bitch-'s car, buy ___

___ my-self a cool ___ gui-tar. ___ I'm gon-na

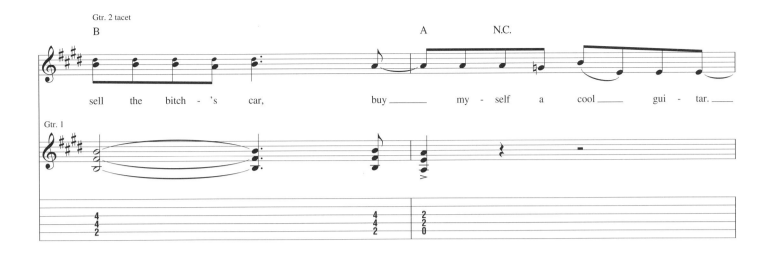

sell the bitch-'s car, buy ___ my-self a cool ___ gui-tar. ___

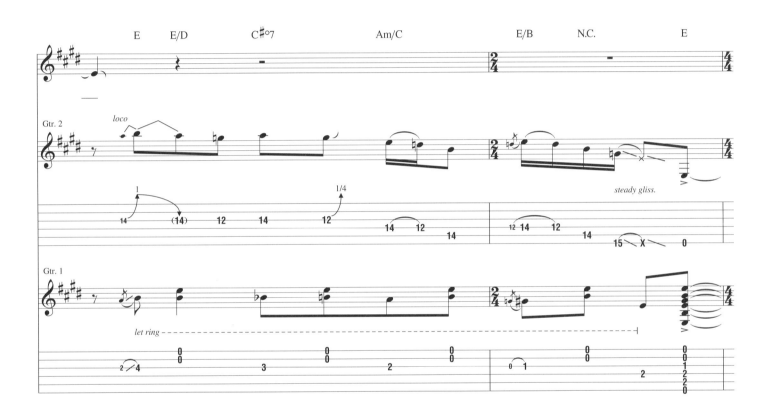

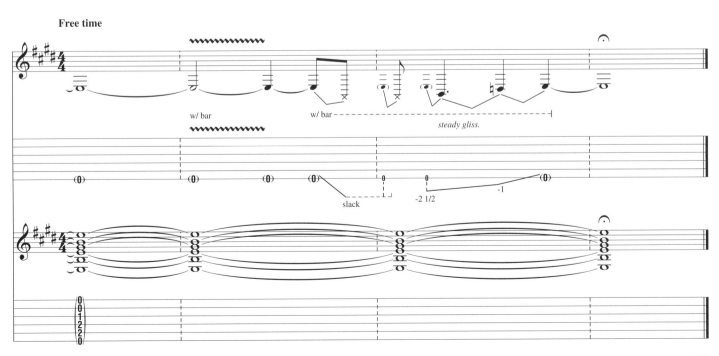

Damn Right, I've Got the Blues

By Buddy Guy

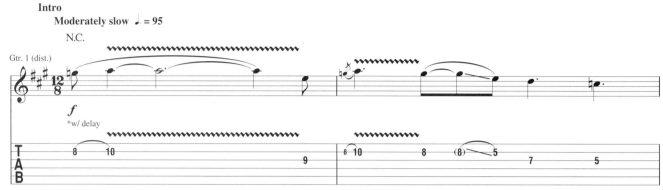

*Set for dotted eighth-note regeneration w/ 1 repeat.

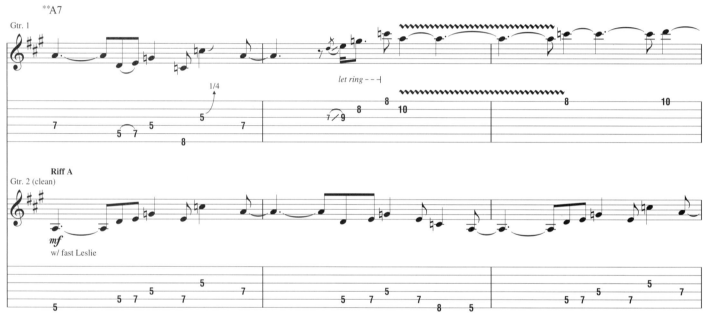

**Chord symbols reflect overall harmony.

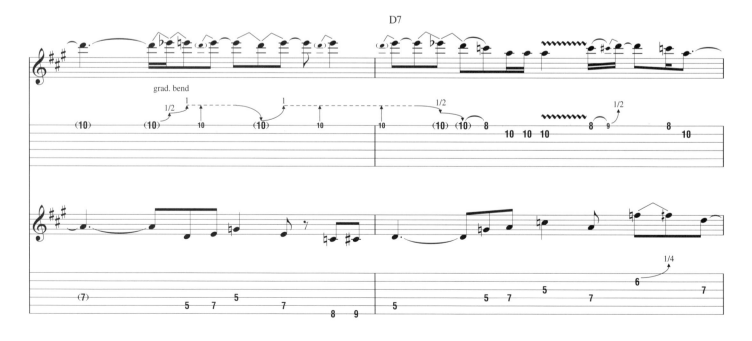

Verse

Gtr. 2: w/ Riff A
2nd time, Gtr. 1 tacet

2nd time, Gtr. 1: w/ Fill 1

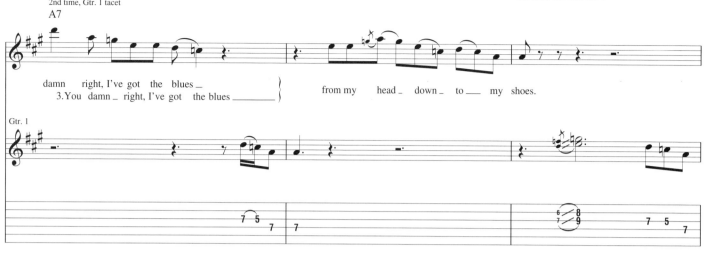

damn right, I've got the blues ___
3. You damn ___ right, I've got the blues _____

from my head ___ down ___ to ___ my shoes.

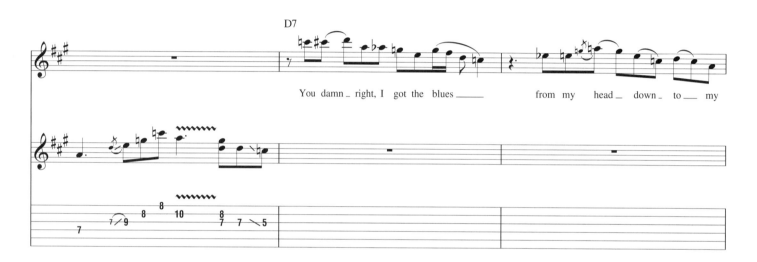

You damn ___ right, I got the blues _____

from my head ___ down ___ to ___ my

To Coda ⊕

2nd time, Gtr. 1: w/ Fill 2

shoes.

I can't ___ win _____

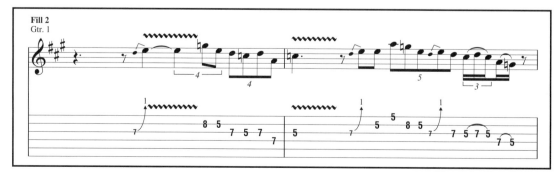

Fill 2
Gtr. 1

Outro
Gtr. 1 tacet
Gtr. 2: w/ Riff B (till fade)

A7

You damn right, I've got the blues.

You damn right, I've got the blues.

Begin fade

You damn right, I got the blues.

Spoken: Yeah.

Gtr. 1

w/ clean tone

Fade out

Dengue Woman Blues

By Jimmie Vaughan

Intro

Free time

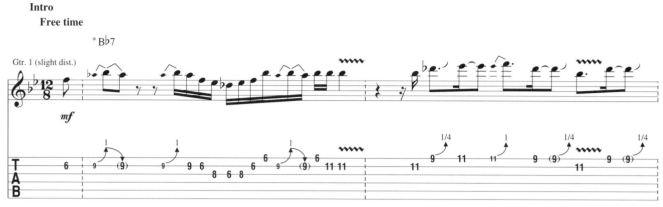

*Chord symbols reflect basic harmony.

Moderately slow ♩. = 60

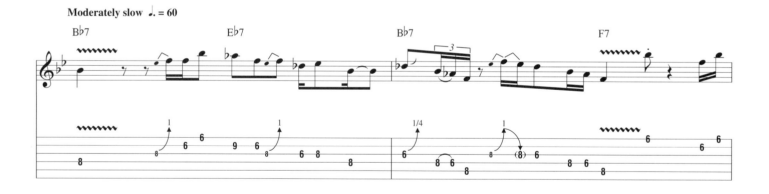

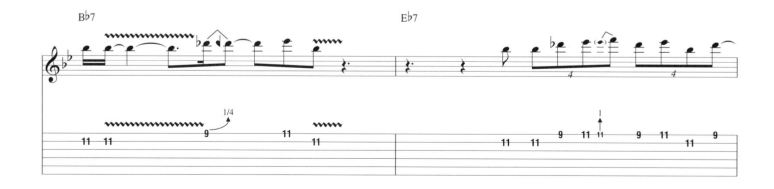

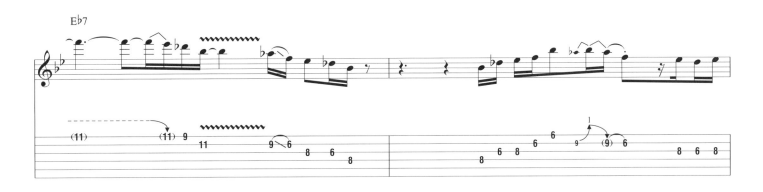

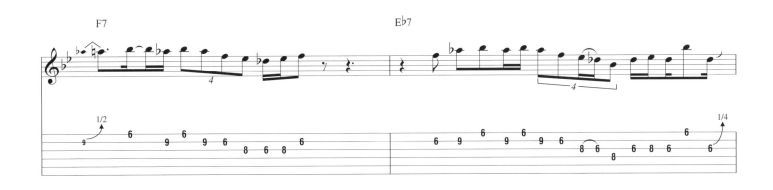

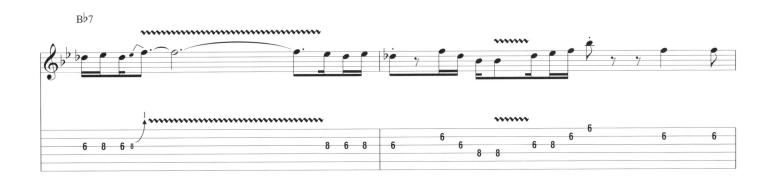

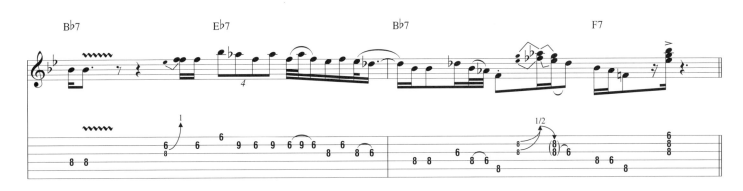

Verse

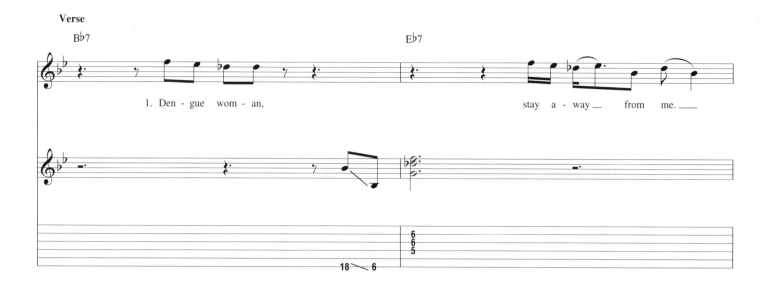

1. Den - gue wom - an,   stay a - way ___ from me. ___

Den - gue wom - an,   stay a - way ___ from me. ___

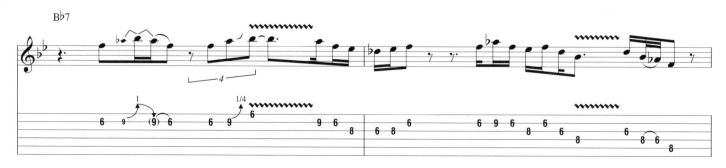

40

You got your fe - ver and your rash ___   all ___ o - ver me. ___

___ That's why   2. That's why

Verse

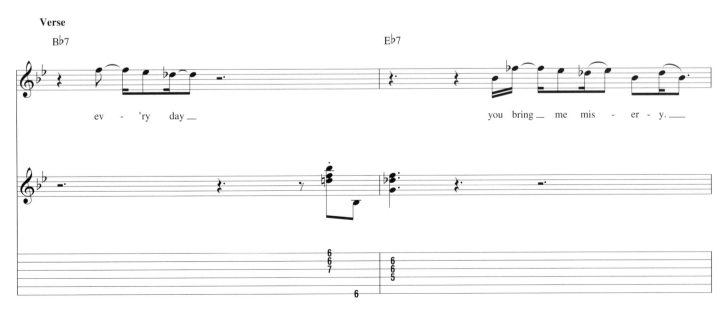

ev - 'ry day ___   you bring ___ me mis - er - y. ___

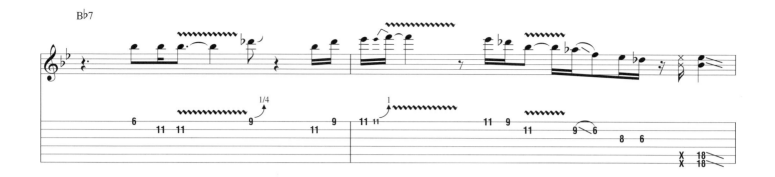

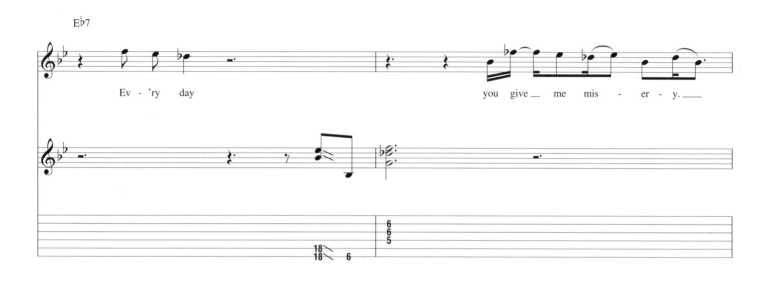

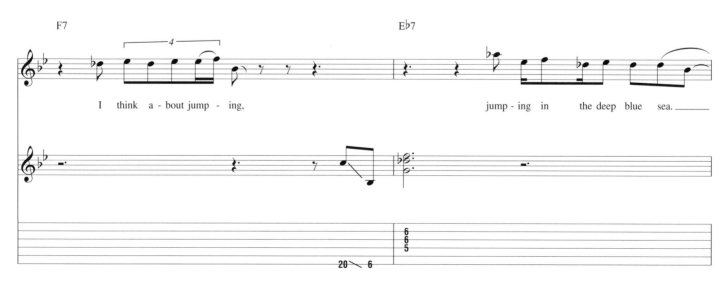

Guitar Solo

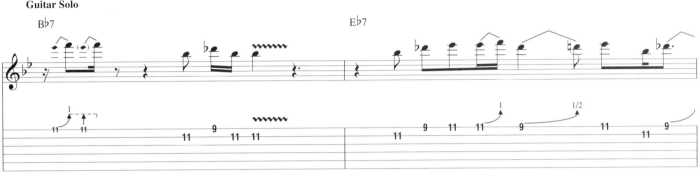

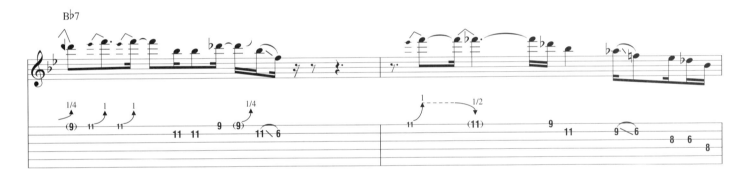

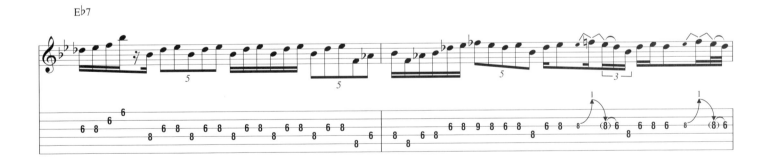

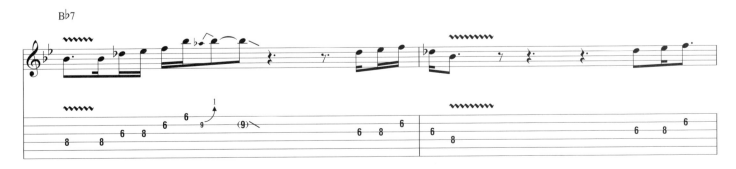

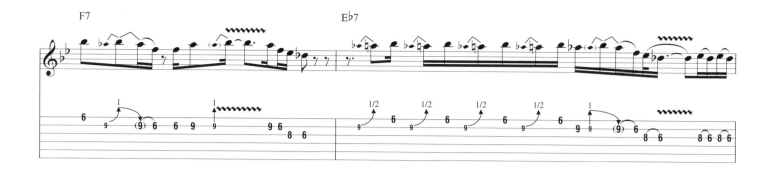

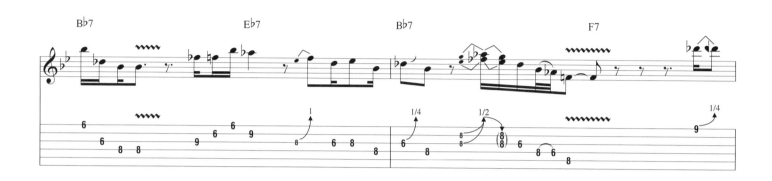

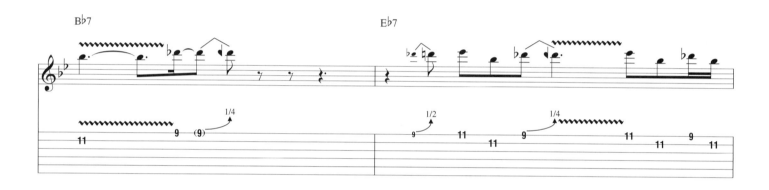

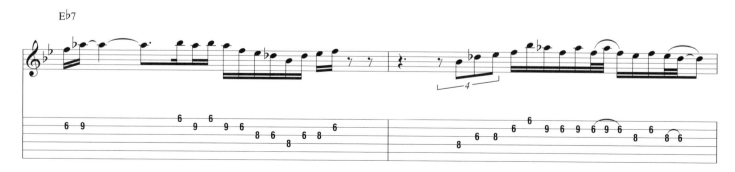

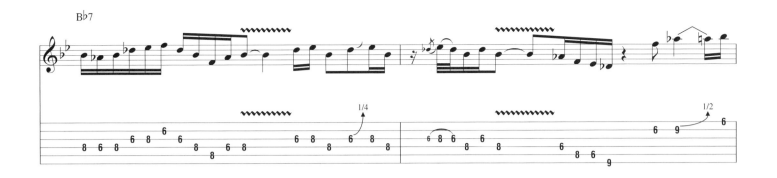

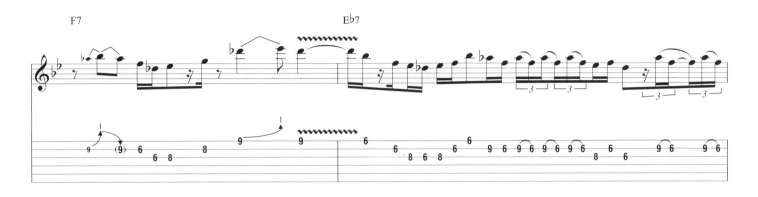

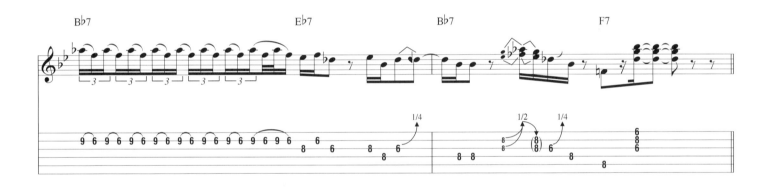

Verse

Gtr. 1 tacet

3. You got me all cra-zy, I can't get out of bed.

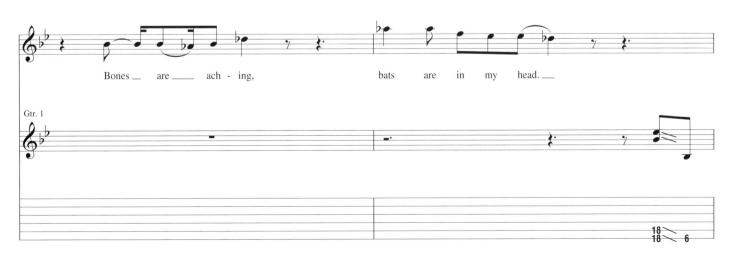

Bones __ are __ ach-ing, bats are in my head. __

Gtr. 1

Outro-Guitar Solo

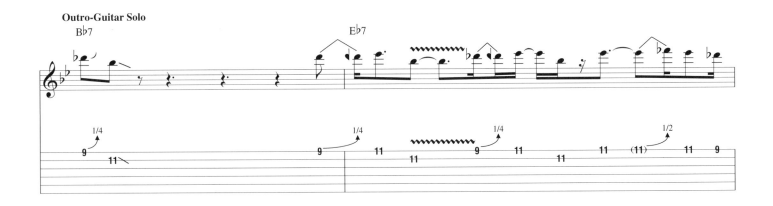

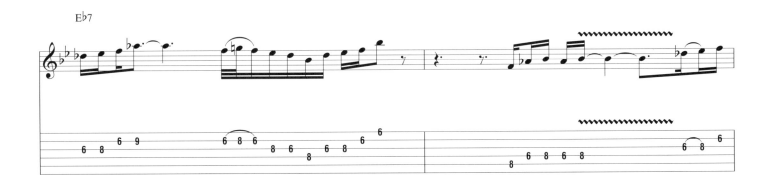

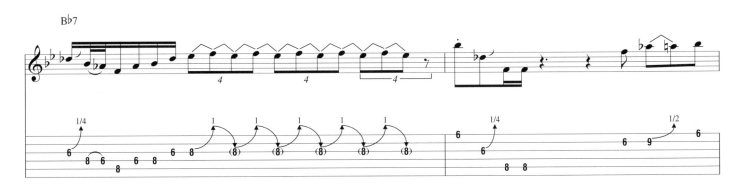

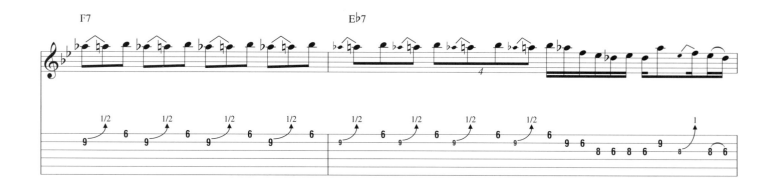

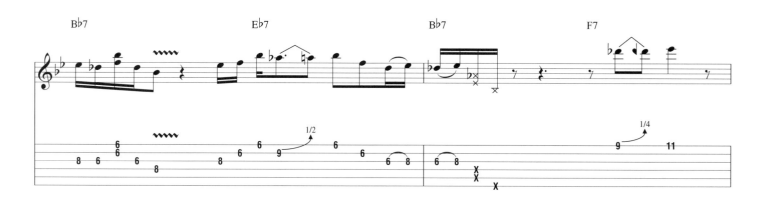

Begin fade

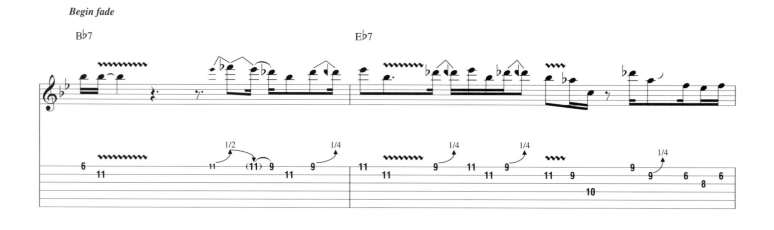

Fade out

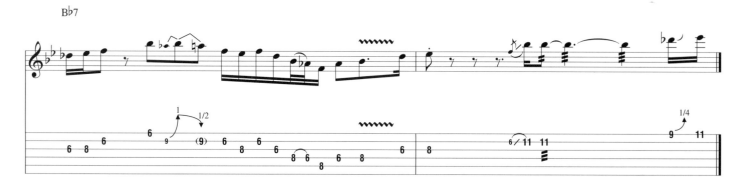

from Stevie Ray Vaughan - *The Sky Is Crying*

Empty Arms

Written by Stevie Ray Vaughan

Tune down 1/2 step:
(low to high) Eb-Ab-Db-Gb-Bb-Eb

Intro-Guitar Solo
Moderately fast Blues ♩ = 152

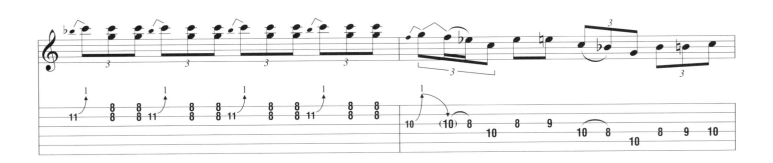

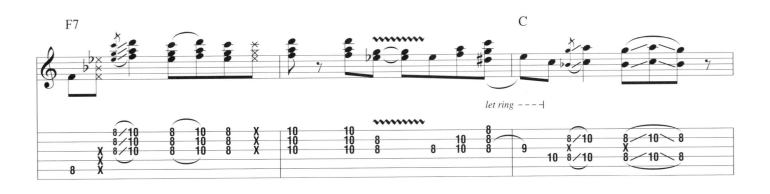

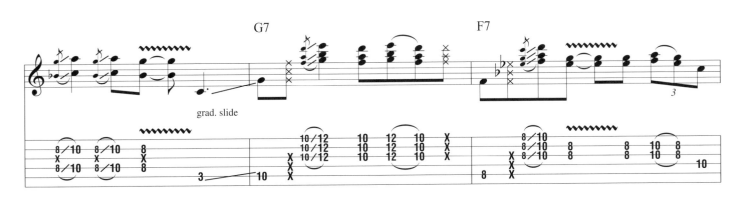

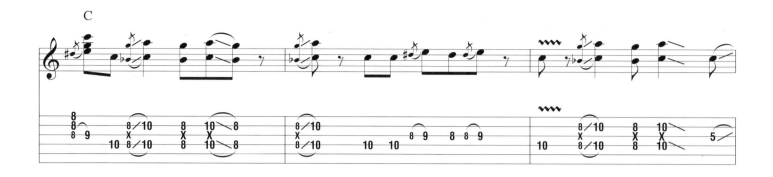

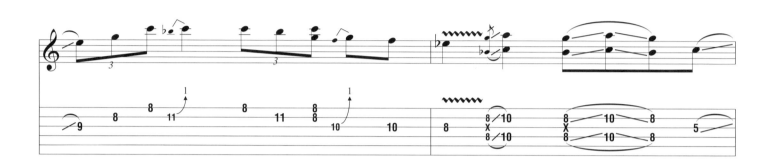

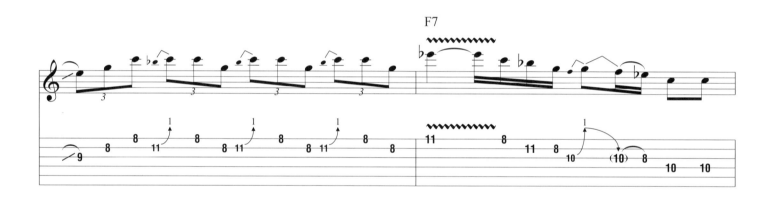

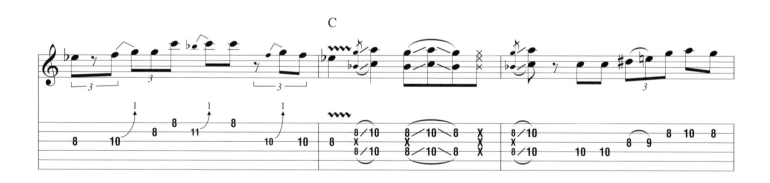

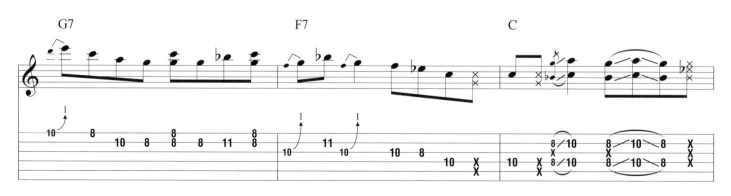

Verse

1. You're gon-na miss ___ me, lit-tle ba - by, the day that I'm gone. ___

rake –

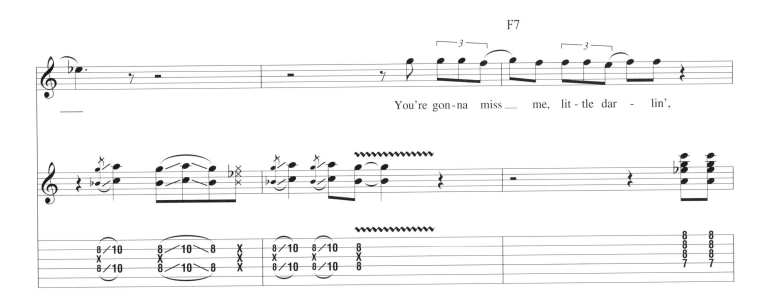

___ You're gon-na miss ___ me, lit-tle dar - lin',

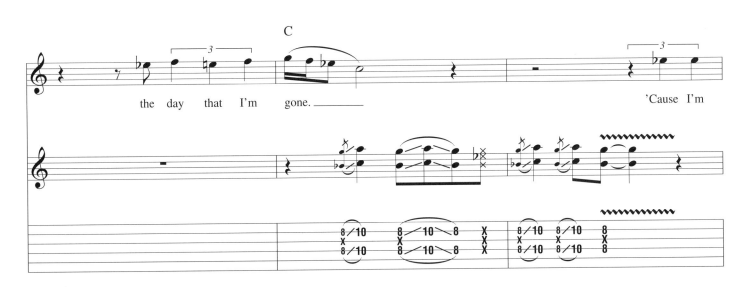

the day that I'm gone. ___ 'Cause I'm

leav-in' in the morn - in', won't be back at all. ____

𝄋 Verse

2. You have run __(4.)__ me rag - ged, ba - by. 'S your own fault __ you're on your
3., 5. *See additional lyrics*

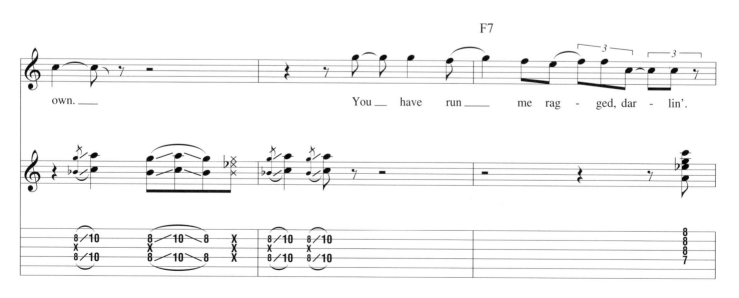

own. ____ You __ have run ____ me rag - ged, dar - lin'.

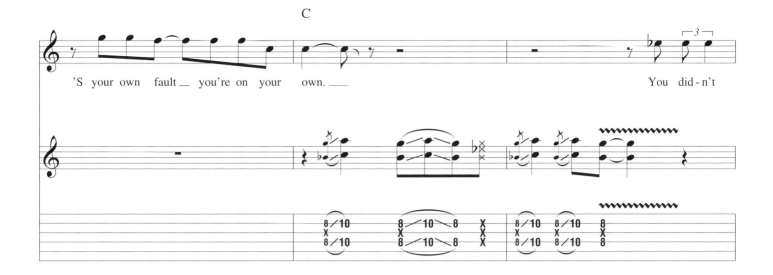

'S your own fault___ you're on your own.___ You did-n't

4th time, To Coda

want me to wait, ba — by, till ___ your oth-er man ___ was gone. ___

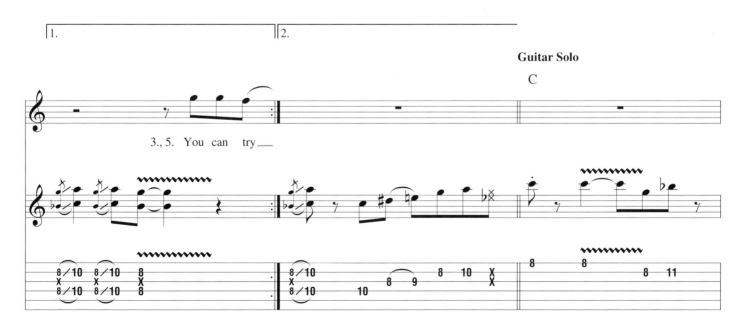

1.   2.

Guitar Solo

3., 5. You can try___

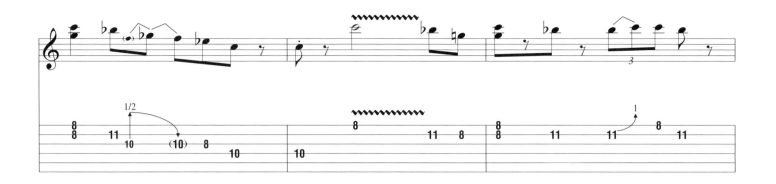

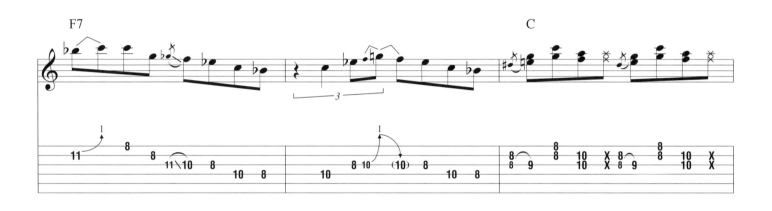

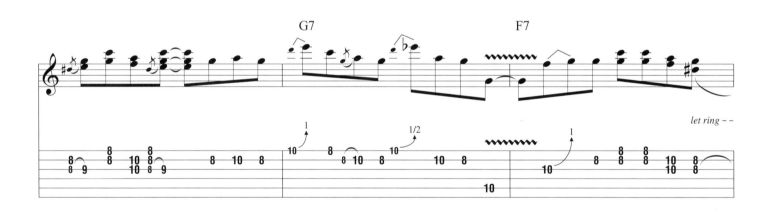

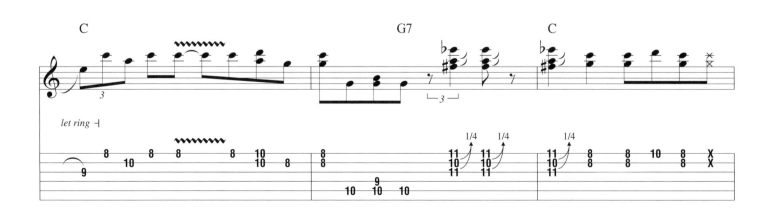

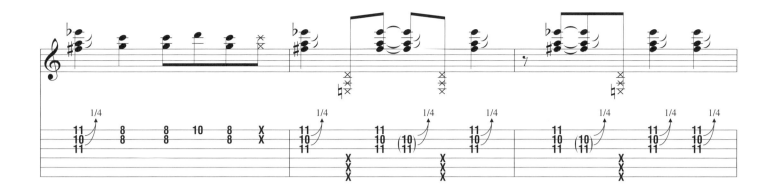

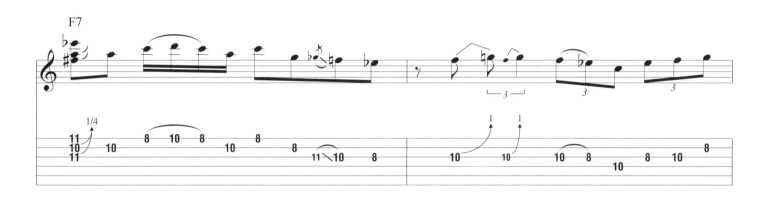

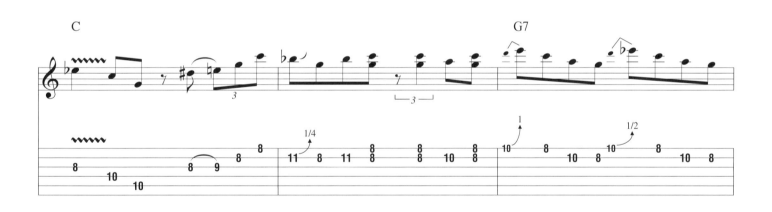

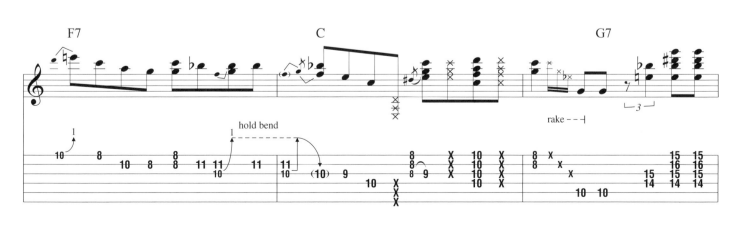

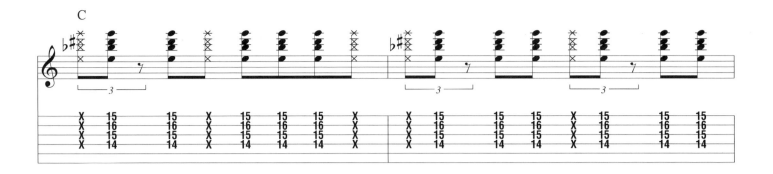

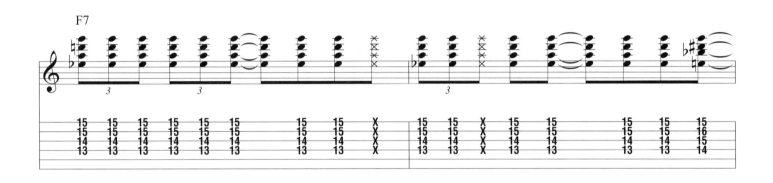

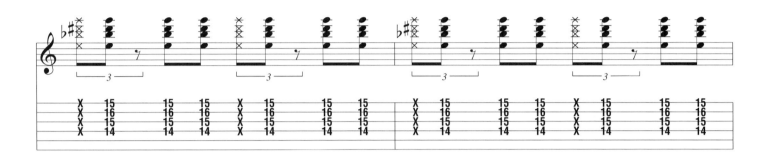

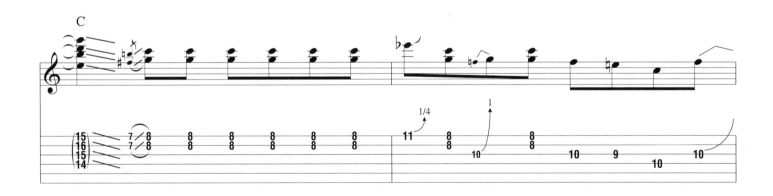

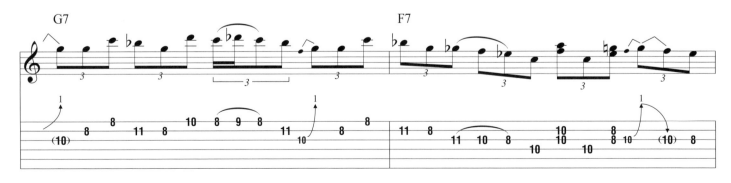

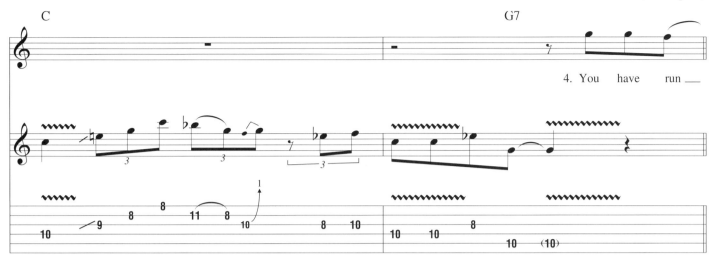

4. You have run ____

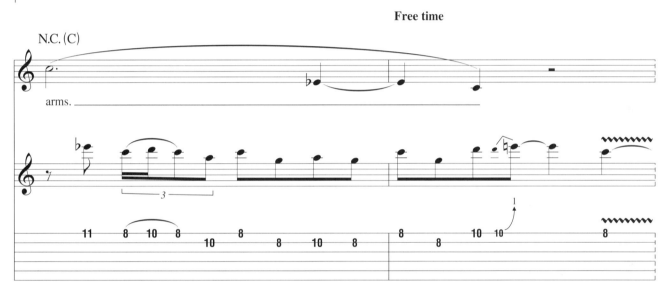

Coda

Free time

arms. ____

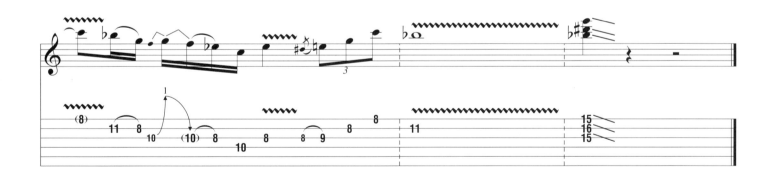

Additional Lyrics

3., 5. You can try to get me back, baby,
With all your tricks and charms.
You can try to get me back, baby,
With all your tricks and charms.
But when all your games are over,
You'll be left with empty arms.

from The Fabulous Thunderbirds - *What's the Word*

Extra Jimmies

By Jimmie Vaughan, Francis Christina and Keith Ferguson

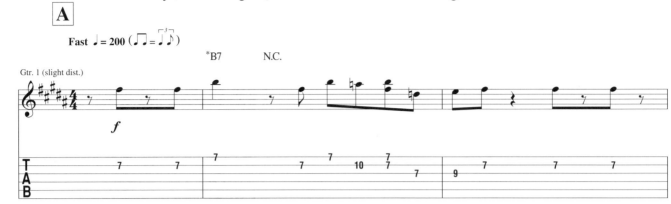

*Chord symbols reflect implied harmony, next 8 meas.

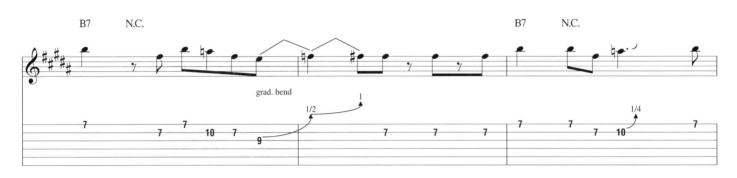

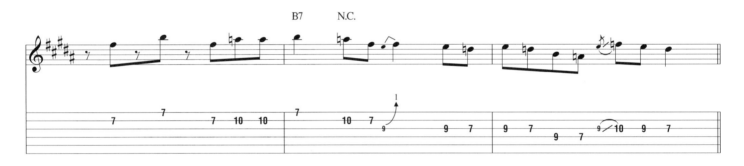

**Chord symbols reflect overall harmony.

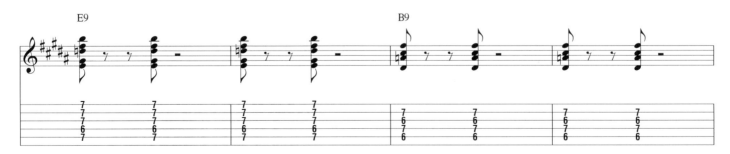

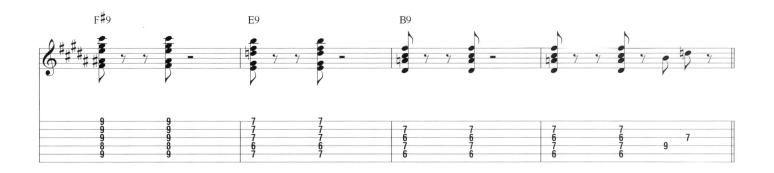

C

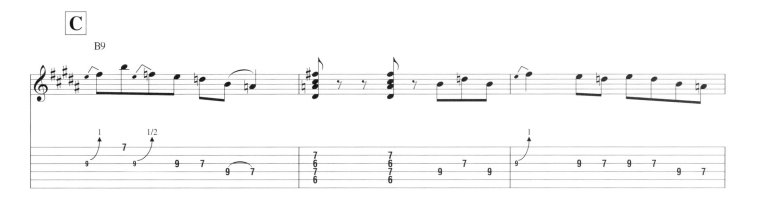

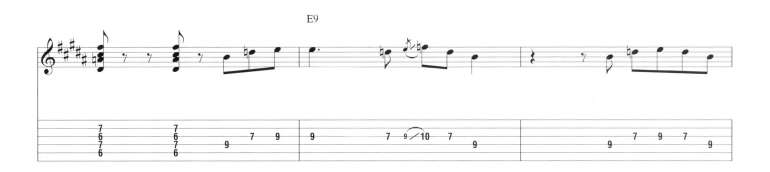

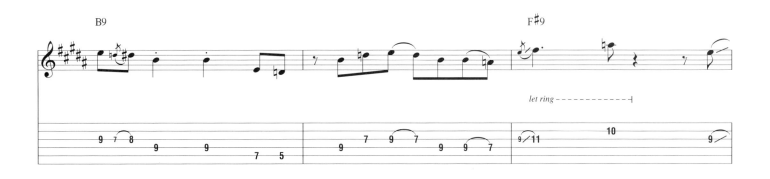

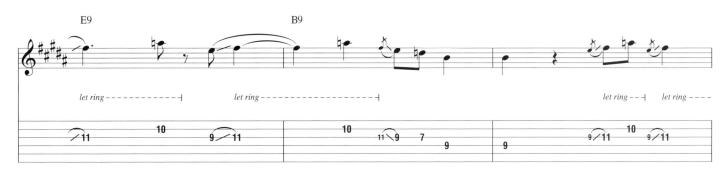

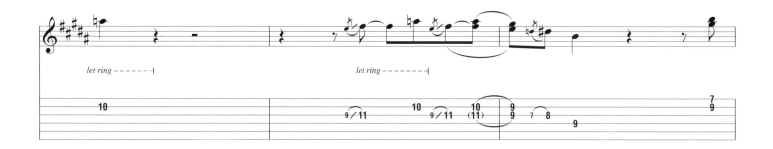

E9

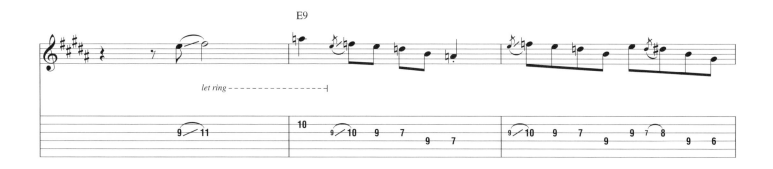

B9   F#9

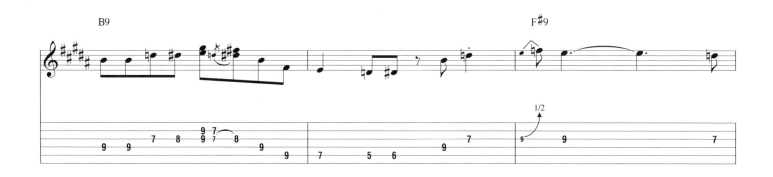

E9   B9

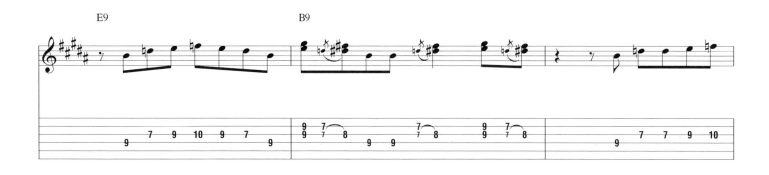

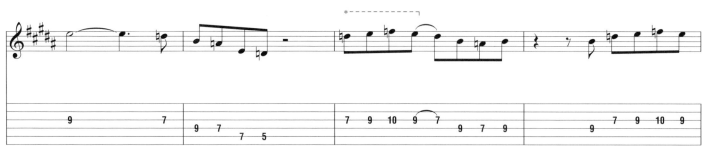

*Played behind the beat.

60

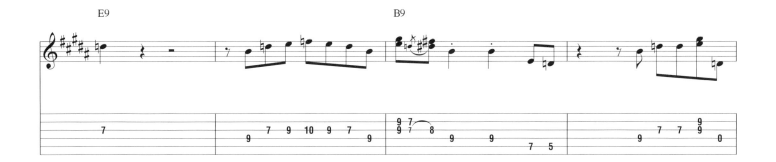

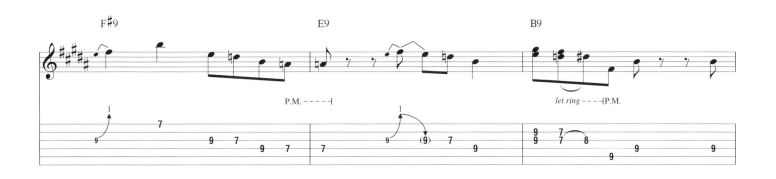

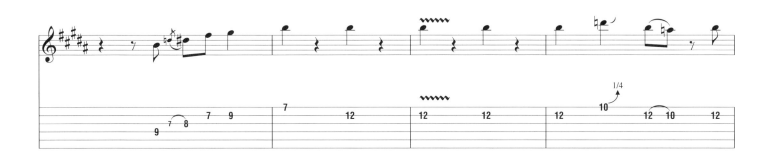

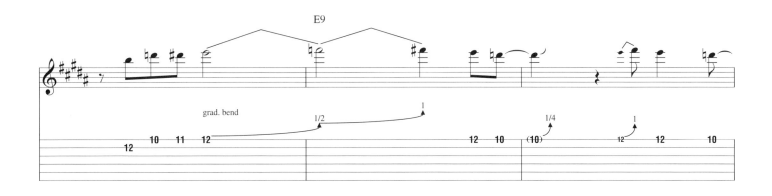

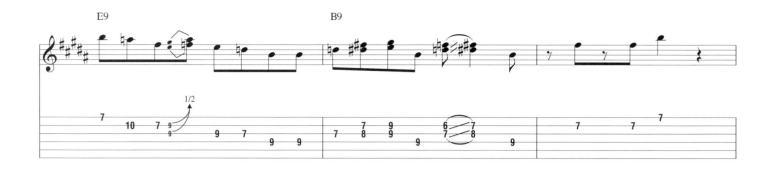

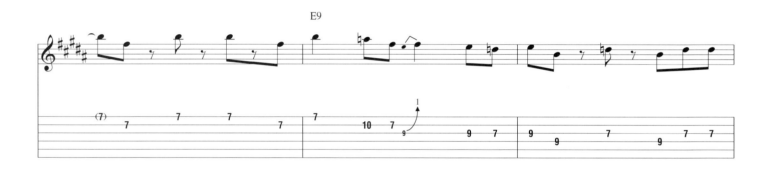

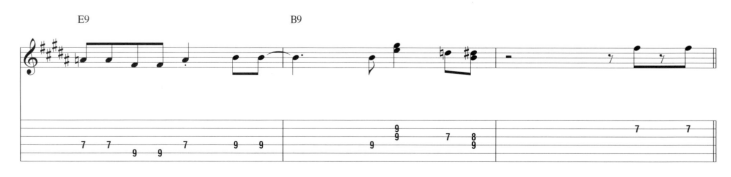

D

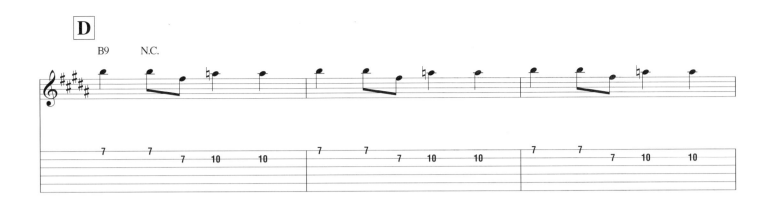

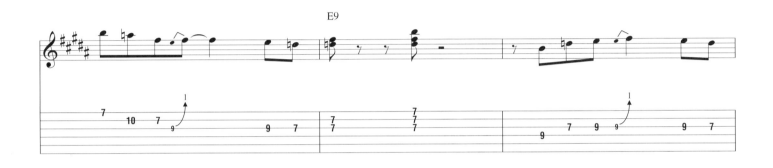

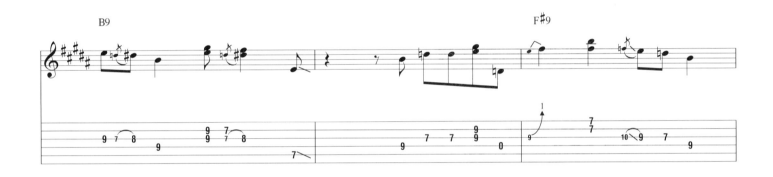

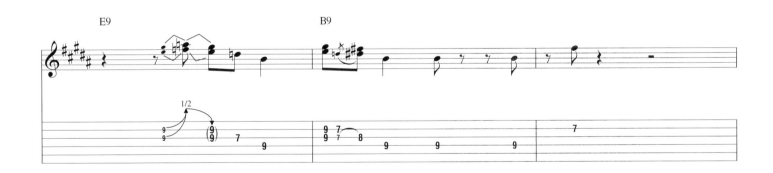

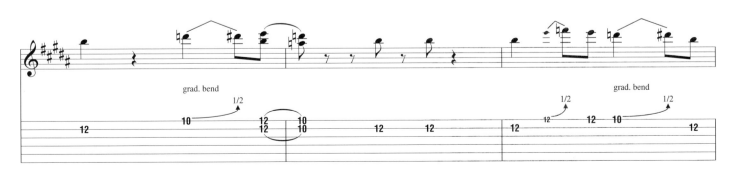

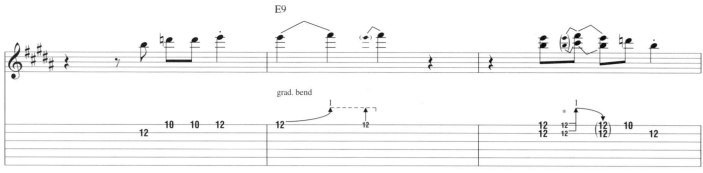

*Catch and bend both strings w/ ring finger.

E

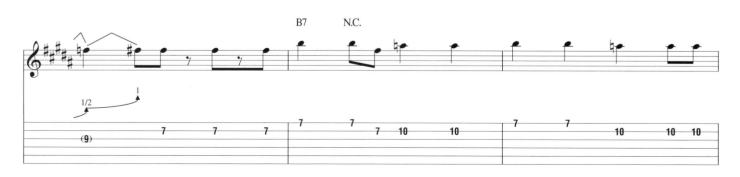

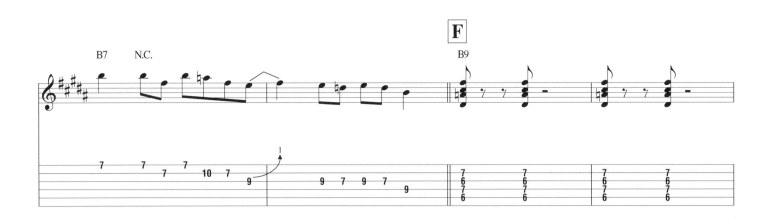

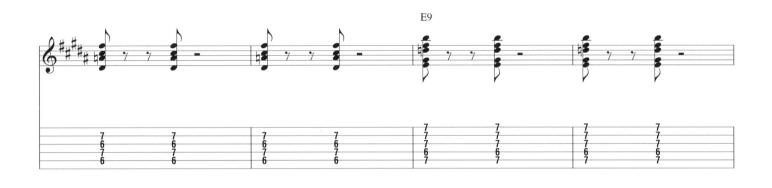

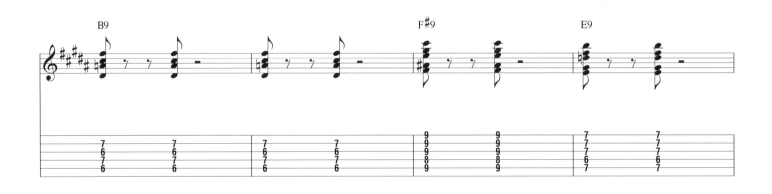

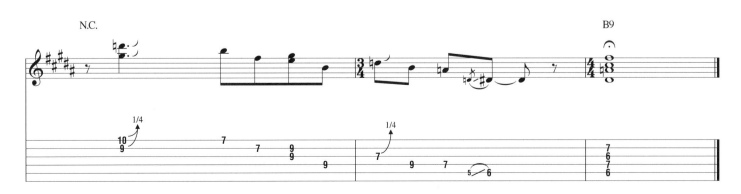

from Tommy Castro - *Painkiller*

A Good Fool Is Hard to Find

Words and Music by Gloria Houston and Nina Shackelford

Intro
Moderately fast ♩ = 140

*Chord symbols reflect overall harmony.

Guitar Solo

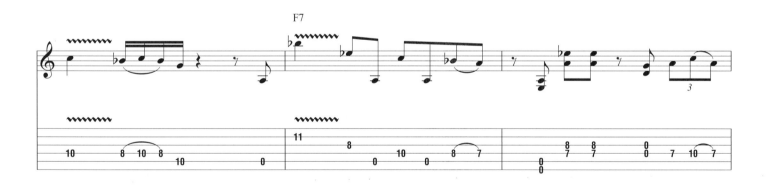

**Gtr. 1 (dist.)

f

**Coco Montoya

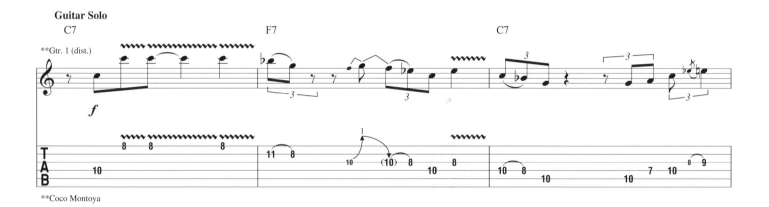

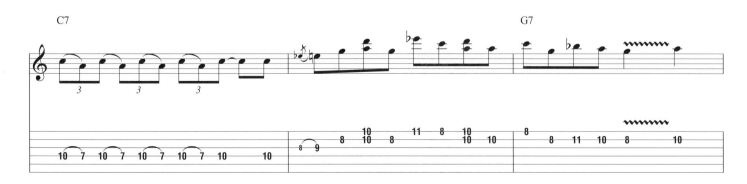

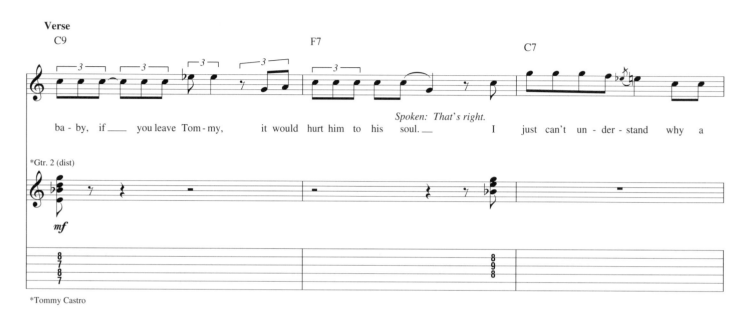

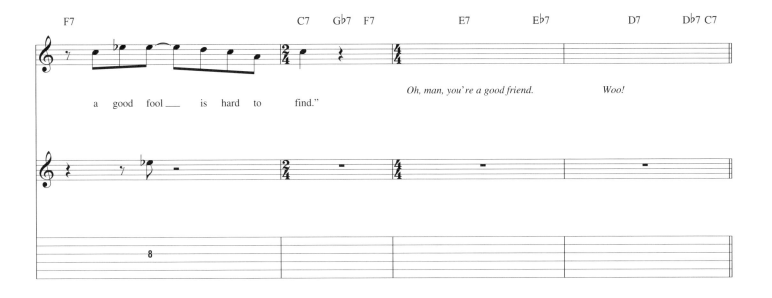

a good fool___ is hard to find."

Oh, man, you're a good friend.   *Woo!*

Guitar Solo

Tommy Castro: I got mad!

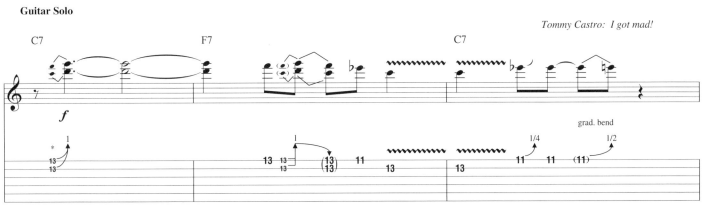

*Catch and bend both strings w/ ring finger.

I got kinda mad.

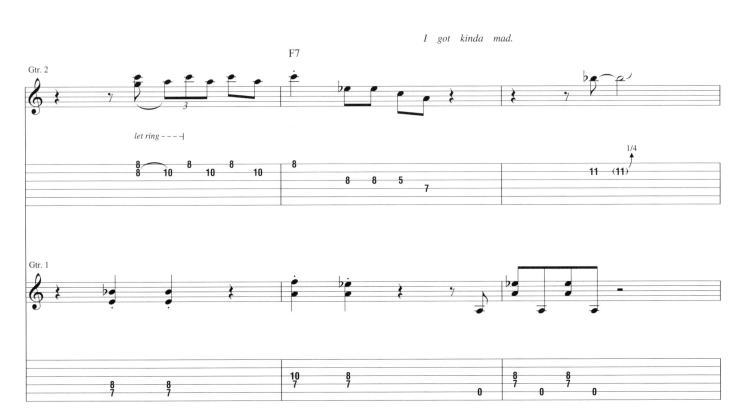

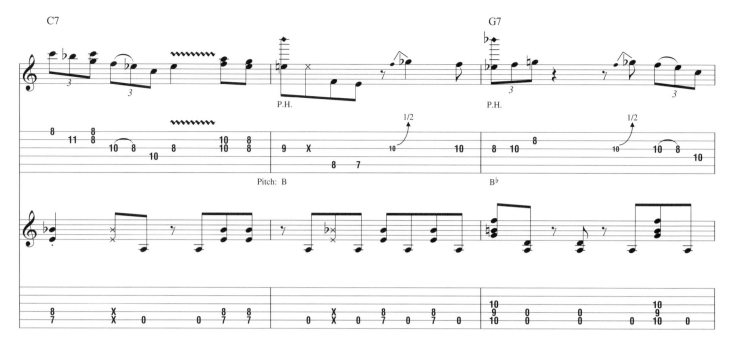

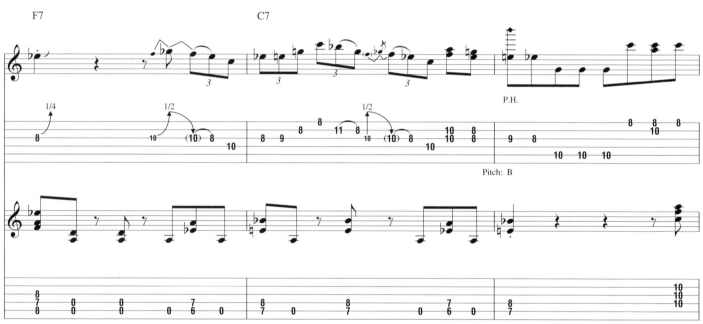

*T = Thumb on 6th string

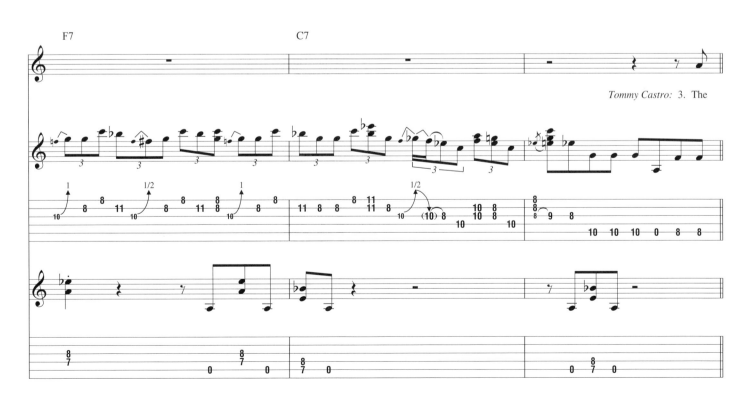

Tommy Castro: 3. The

Verse

last time ___ she left me   I   did-n't have much ___ to lose; ___   she   left me noth-in', Co - co, but a pair

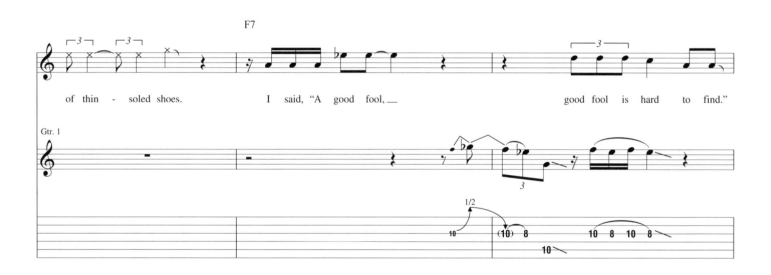

of thin - soled shoes.   I   said, "A   good fool, ___   good fool   is hard   to find."

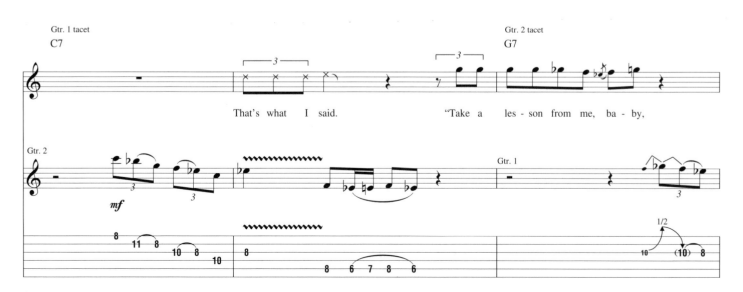

That's what   I   said.   "Take a   les - son from me, ba - by,

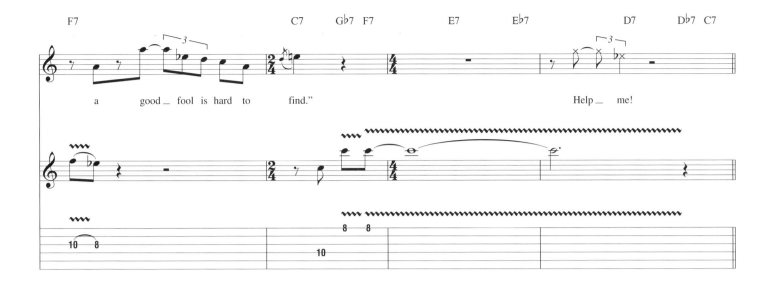

a good fool is hard to find." Help me!

Guitar Solo

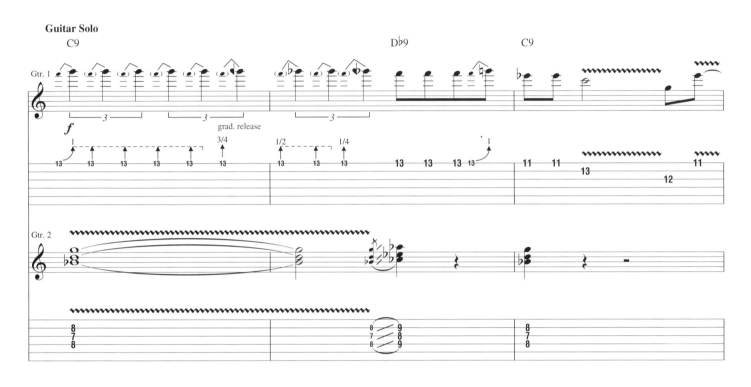

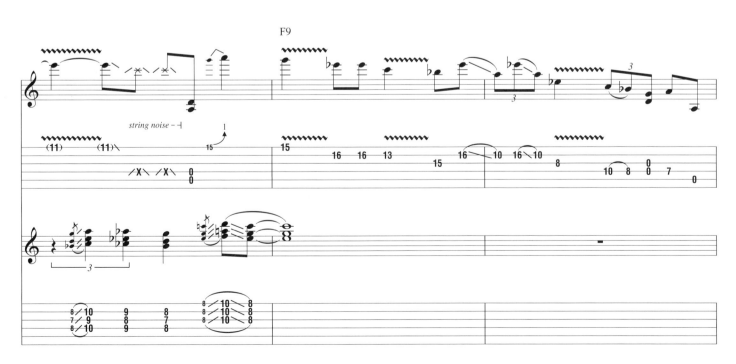

Verse

Gtr. 2 tacet

Coco Montoya:
4. "Lis - ten to me, ba - by, I think you should be told, _ when they made your man Tom - my,

Gtr. 1

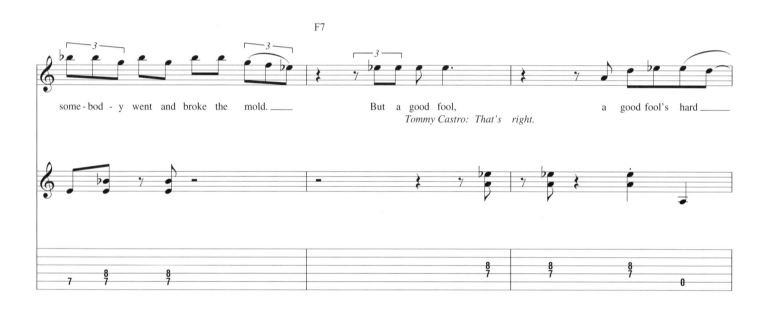

some - bod - y went and broke the mold. _____ But a good fool, a good fool's hard _____

Tommy Castro: That's right.

_____ to find. _____ Take a les - son from me, ba - by, _____

You better listen!

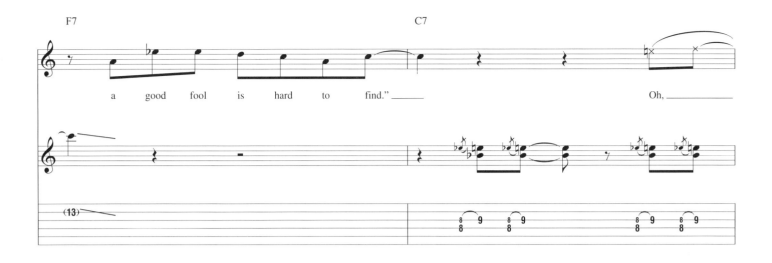

a   good   fool   is   hard   to   find." _____   Oh, _____

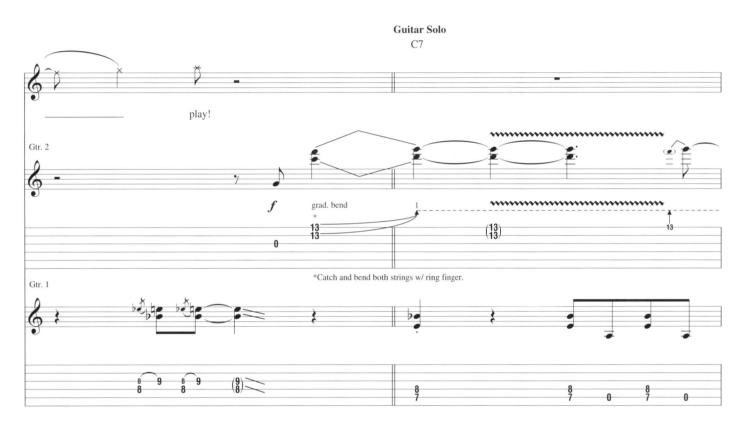

Guitar Solo

_____ play!

Gtr. 2

*Catch and bend both strings w/ ring finger.

Gtr. 1

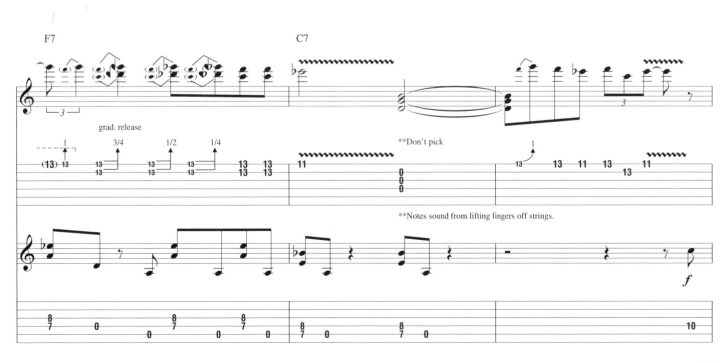

**Don't pick

**Notes sound from lifting fingers off strings.

*Catch and bend both strings w/ ring finger.

Interlude

Gtr. 2 tacet

Coco Montoya: Spoken: Hey, Tommy.   Let me tell you something.   I'll tell you what we're gonna do.
          Tommy Castro: Spoken: Yeah,   man!

We're gonna go home and get ourselves right.   We're gonna go step out tonight   and go down to
                                                                              Yeah.

downtown   San   Francisco   and   I   know   we're   gonna   find   at   least   two   or

three   or   four,   five,   six,   seven, eight, nine,

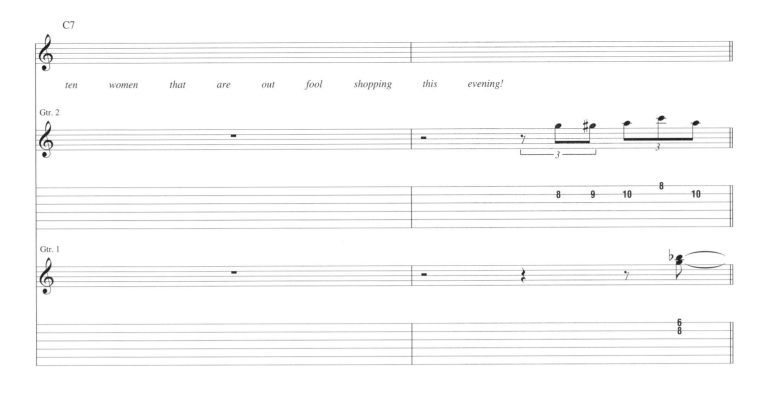

ten women that are out fool shopping this evening!

Outro-Guitar Solo

w/ talking ad lib.

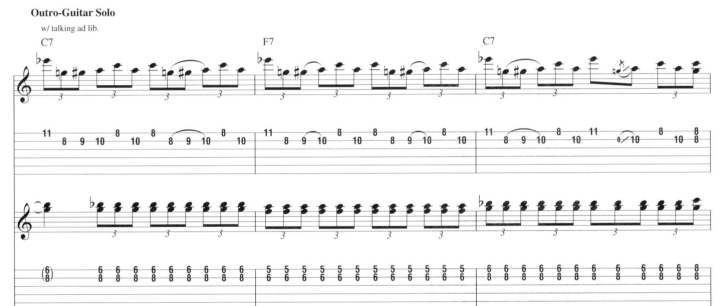

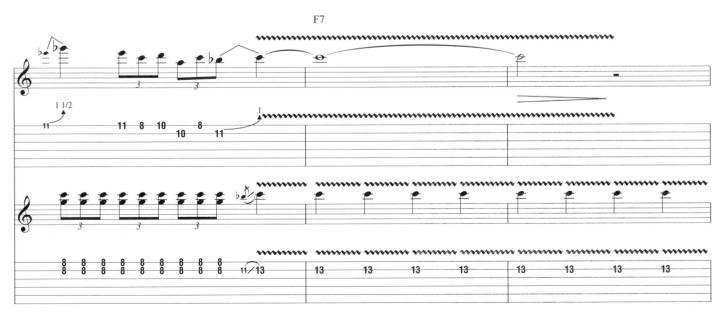

from Eric Clapton - *From the Cradle*

I'm Tore Down
Words and Music by Sonny Thompson

*Chord symbols reflect basic harmony.

tore down, al - most lev - el with the ground. __ Why'd ___ I

feel _ like this _ when _ my ba - by can't be found? _ 2. I

℁ Verse
Gtr. 1 tacet

love you babe _ with all my heart _ and soul. _ Love like mine _ will nev - er grow old.
3. Love you ba - by with all ___ my might. _ Love like mine _ is out - ta sight. I'll

Chorus

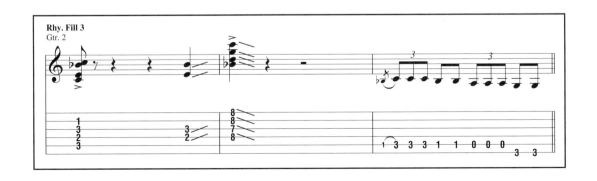

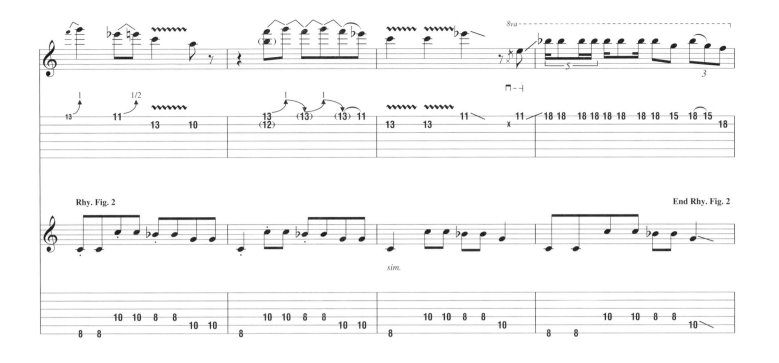

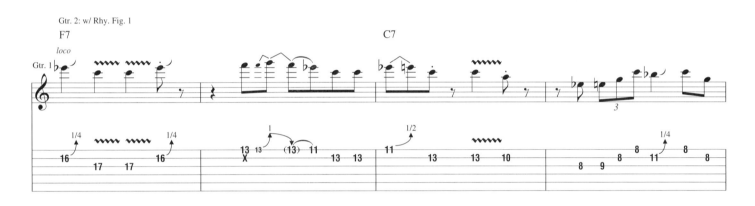

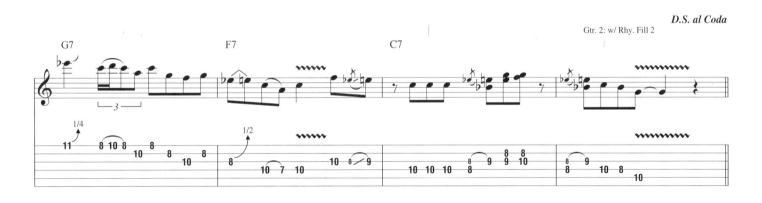

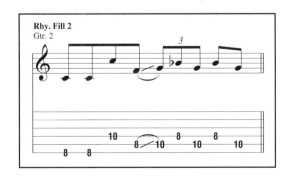

Coda

Chorus
Gtr. 2: w/ Rhy. Fig. 1

tore down. ___ I'm al - most lev - el with the ground. ___

Why'd I feel ___ like this ___ when ___ my ba - by can't be found?

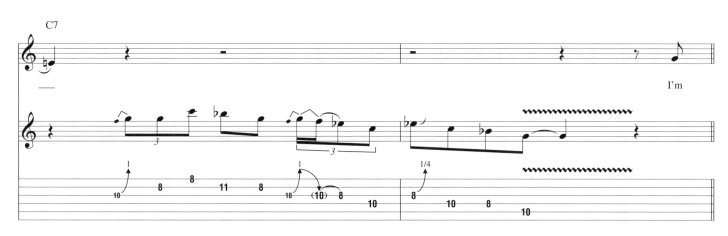

___ I'm

Outro-Chorus
Gtr. 2: w/ Rhy. Fig. 2

tore down ___ al - most lev - el with the ground. ___ Well, I'm

Lie to Me

Words and Music by David Rivkin and Bruce McCabe

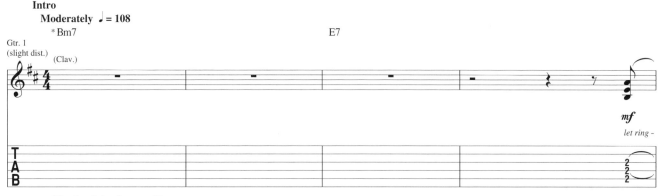

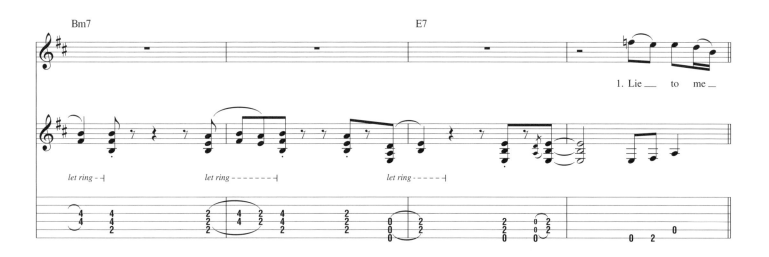

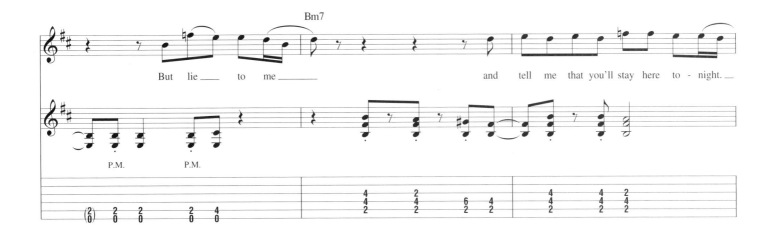

But lie ___ to me ___ and tell me that you'll stay here to - night. ___

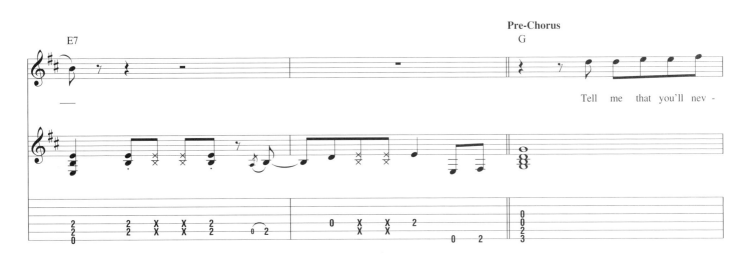

Tell me that you'll nev -

er leave, oh, ___ and I just try ___ to make be - lieve ___

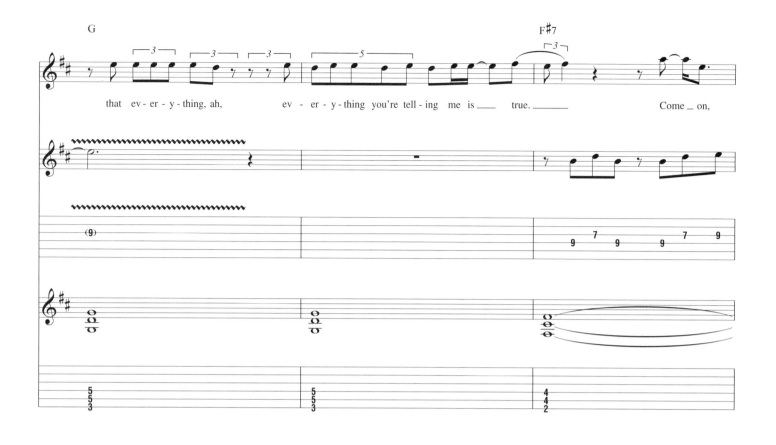

that ev-er-y-thing, ah,   ev-er-y-thing you're tell-ing me is ___ true. ___   Come ___ on,

Chorus

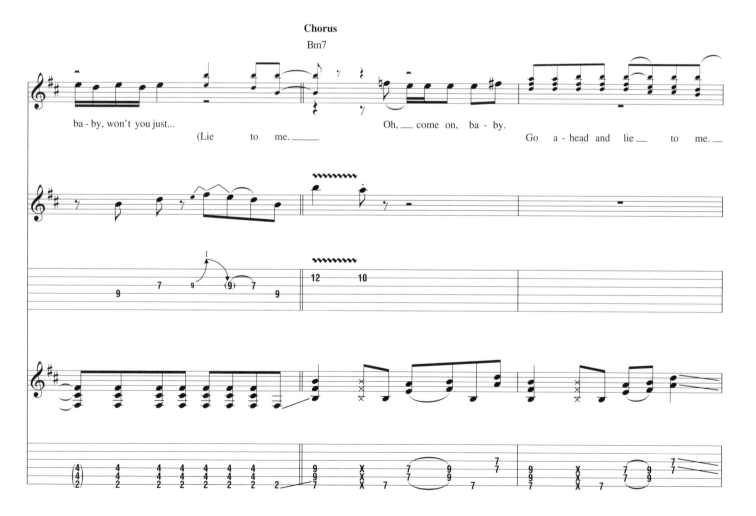

ba - by, won't you just...   Oh, ___ come on, ba - by.
(Lie   to   me. ___)   Go a - head and lie ___ to me. ___

Yeah, ___ lie to me. Know what I'm talk - ing a - bout.
Oh, ___ won't you lie to me, ___ yeah.

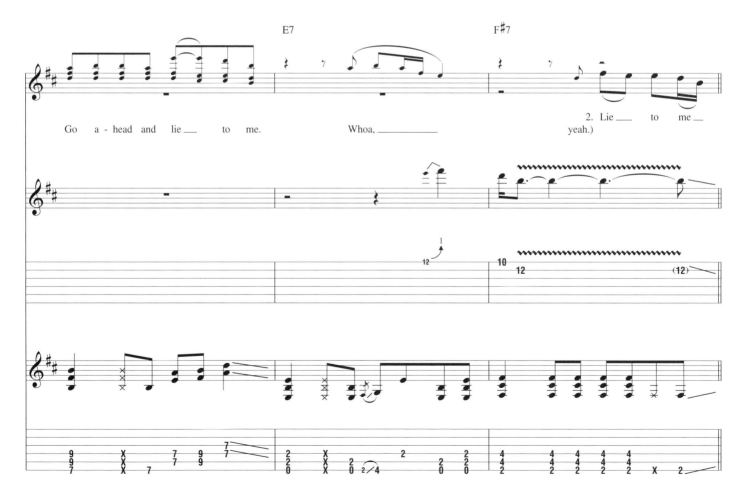

Go a - head and lie ___ to me. Whoa, _____ 2. Lie ___ to me ___ yeah.)

Verse

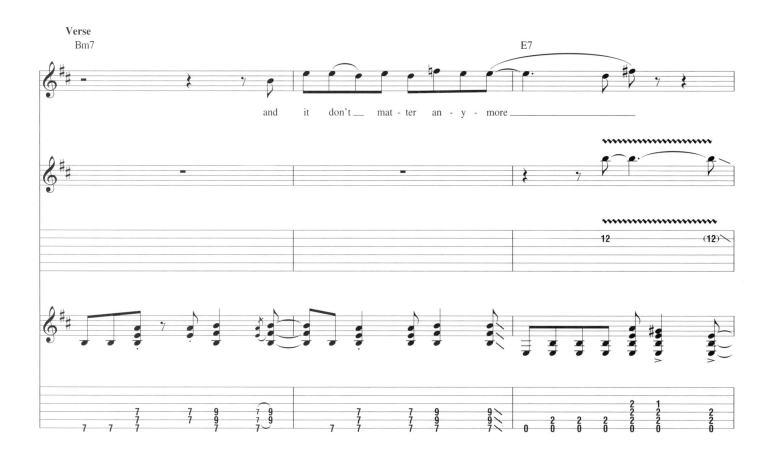

and it don't __ mat-ter an-y-more _____

and it could nev - er be _____   the way it was   be - fore. __

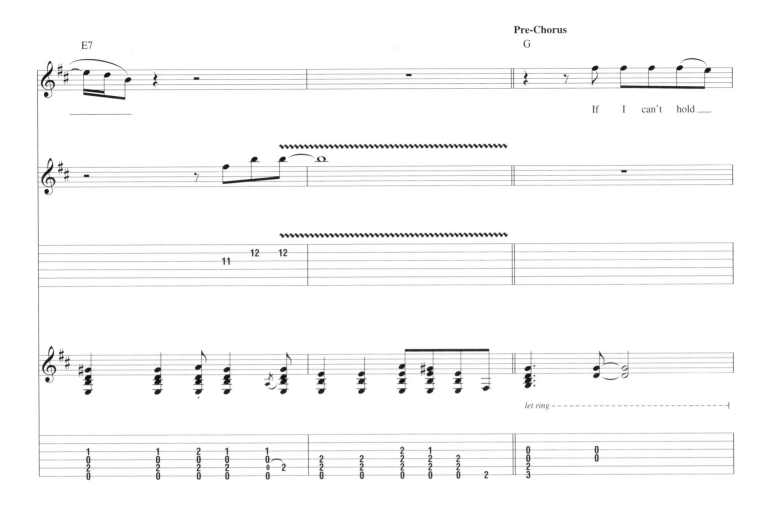

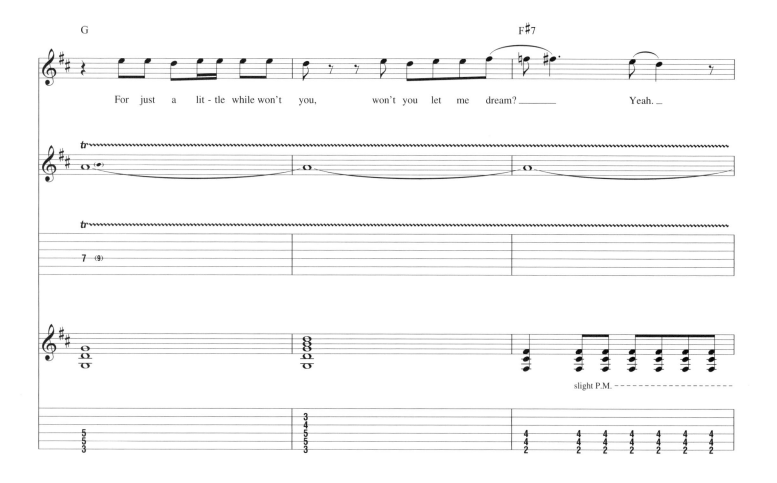

For just a lit - tle while won't you, won't you let me dream? _____ Yeah. _

Guitar Solo

Come on and...

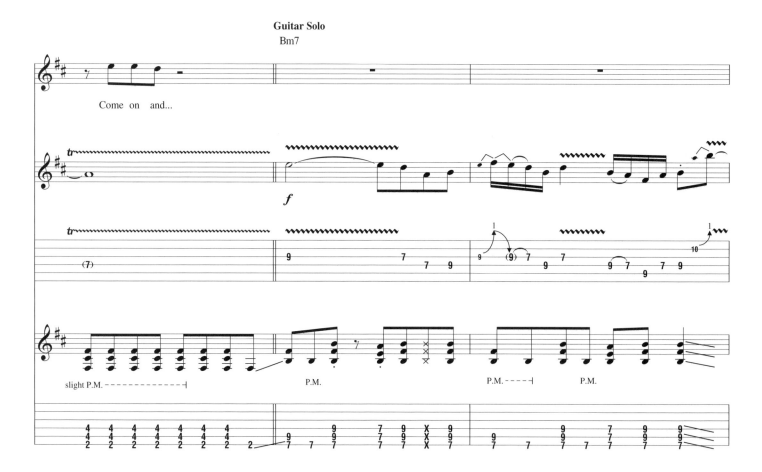

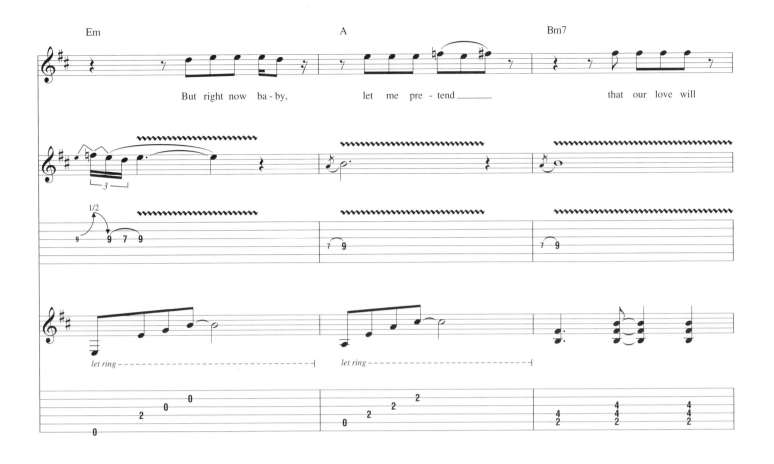

But right now ba-by,   let me pre-tend_____   that our love will

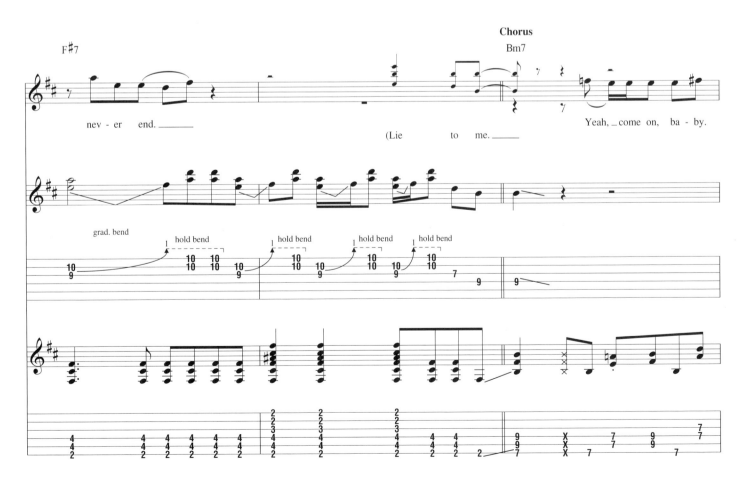

nev-er end._____   Yeah,_ come on, ba-by.

(Lie   to   me._____

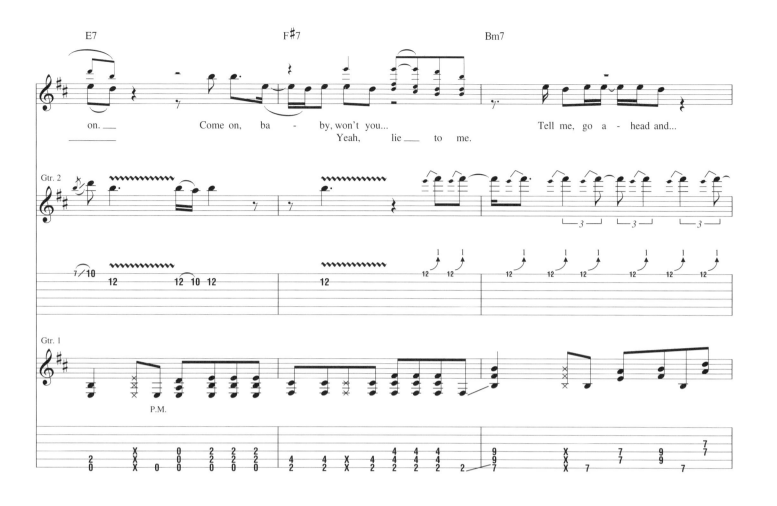

on. ___   Come on, ba - by, won't you...   Tell me, go a - head and...

Yeah, lie ___ to me.

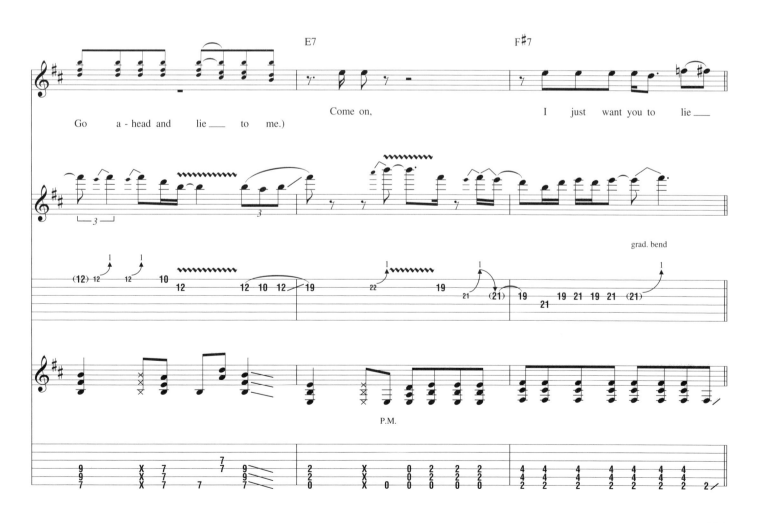

Go a - head and lie ___ to me.)   Come on,   I just want you to lie ___

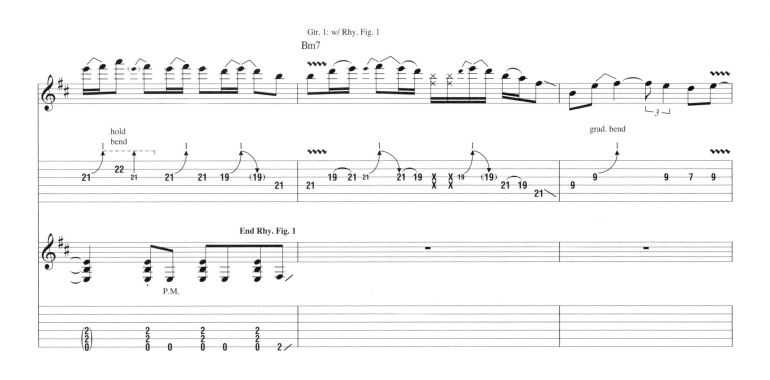

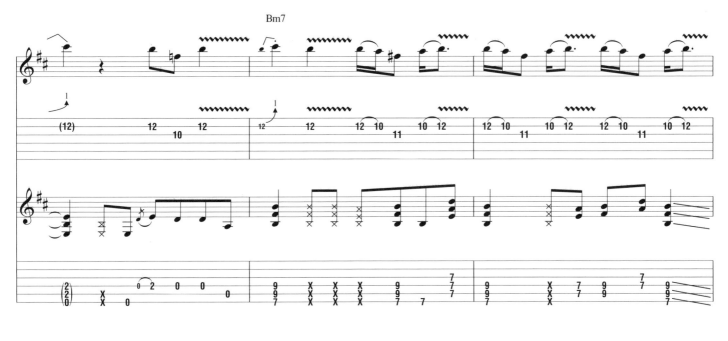

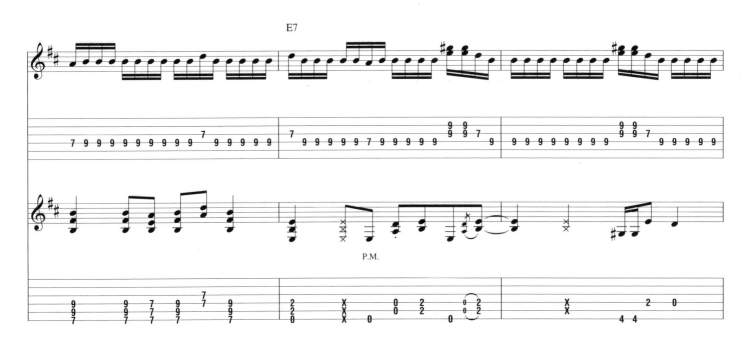

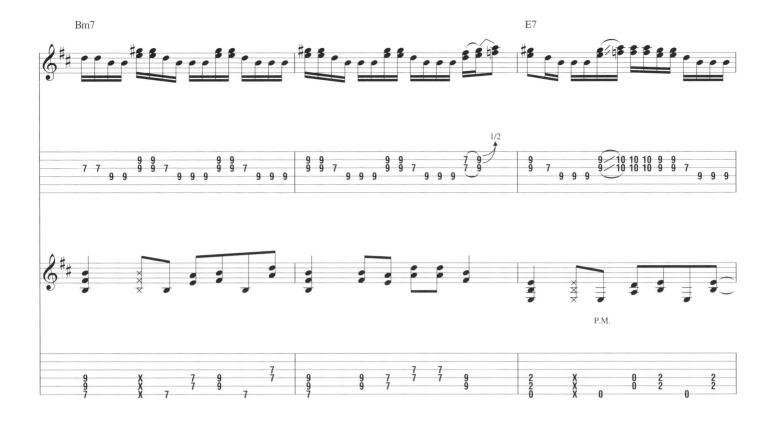

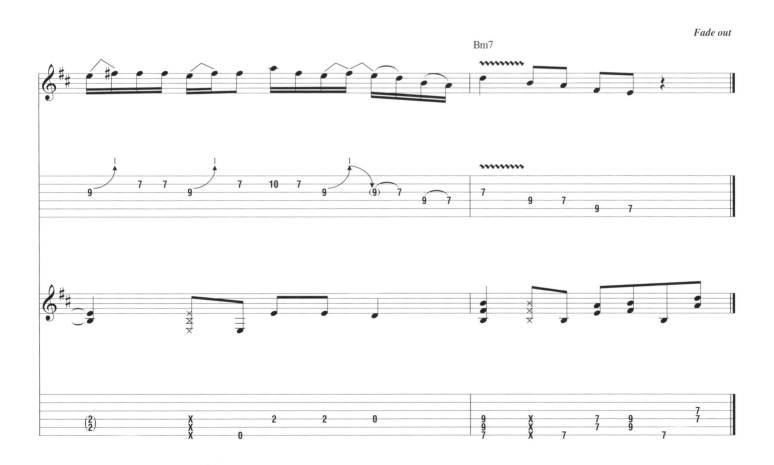

from Chris Duarte Group - *Texas Sugar/Strat Magik*

My Way Down

Words and Music by Chris Duarte and John Jordan

Tune down 1/2 step:
(low to high) E♭-A♭-D♭-G♭-B♭-E♭

Intro
Moderately ♩ = 98

N.C.   **Cm7

Gtr. 1 (slight dist.)

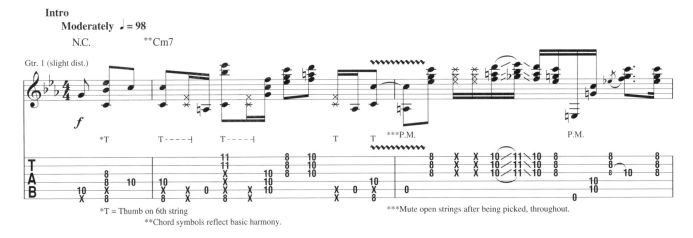

*T = Thumb on 6th string
**Chord symbols reflect basic harmony.

***Mute open strings after being picked, throughout.

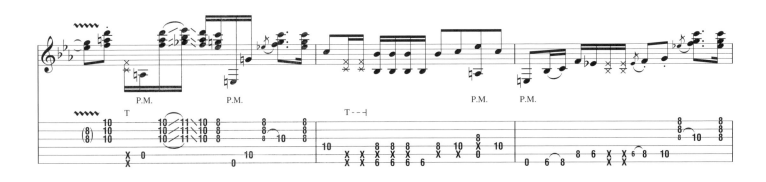

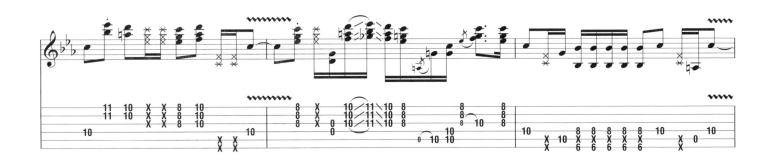

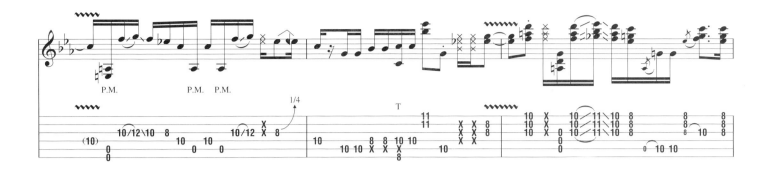

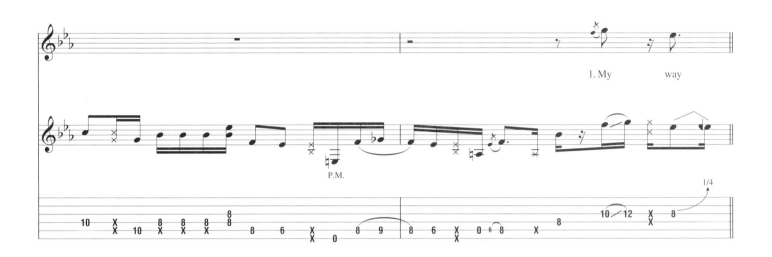

1. My way

Verse

Cm7

down   ain't gon-na be   nice.   Long   road down,

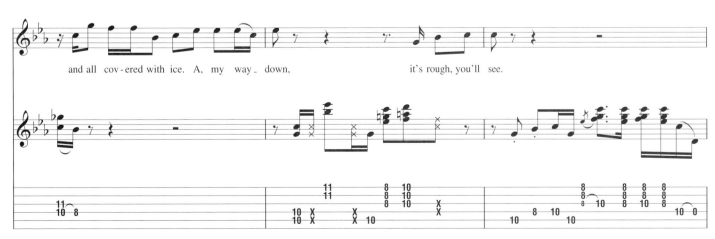

and all cov-ered with ice. A, my way down,   it's rough, you'll see.

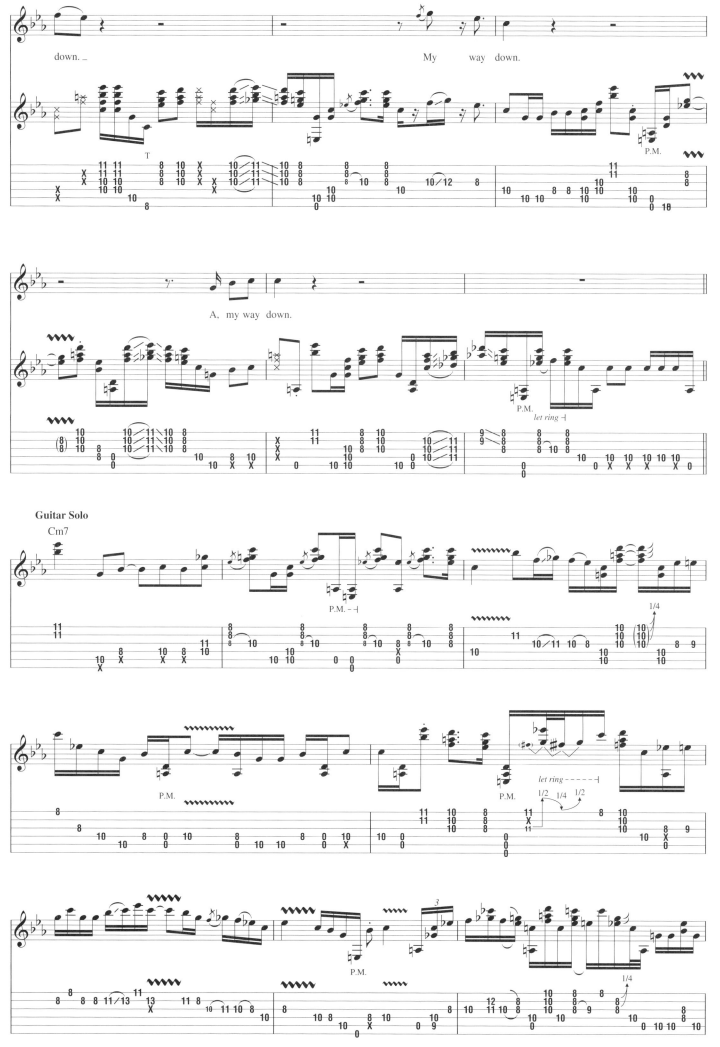

Guitar Solo

Gtr. 2 tacet

Pitch: D♭

*Microphonic fdbk., not caused by string vibration.

**w/ wah-wah

**As filter

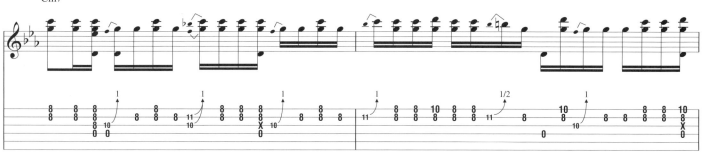

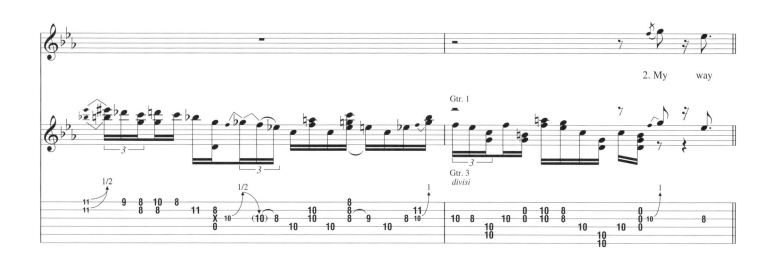

Verse

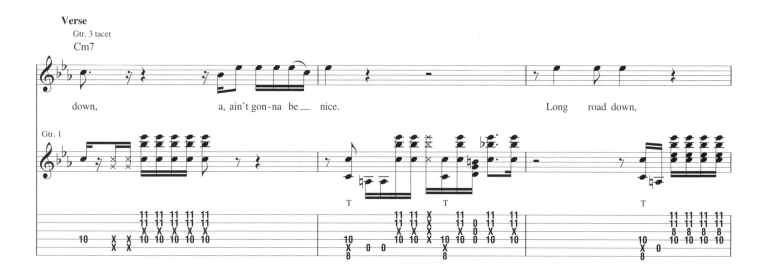

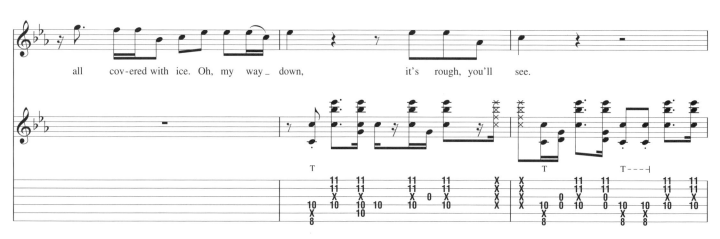

Oh, all the trou-bles I threw off   com-in' back at me.

Crowds get-tin' small - er,   ex - pec - ta - tions grow-in' tall - er.

All this pres - sure on me,   tell me what I got - ta be.

Don't know what I did wrong   to make my jour-ney so ___ long. I

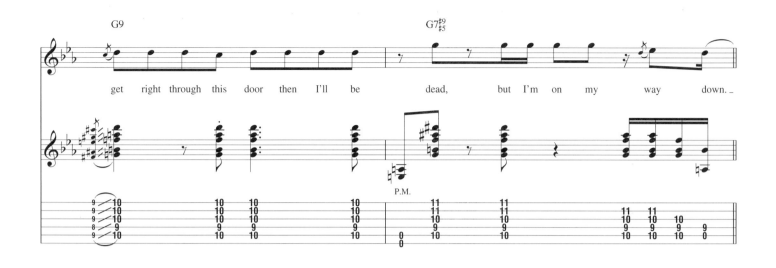

get right through this door then I'll be dead, but I'm on my way down.

Chorus

A, my way down.

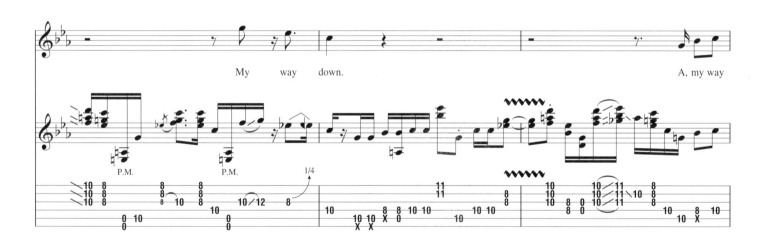

My way down.   A, my way

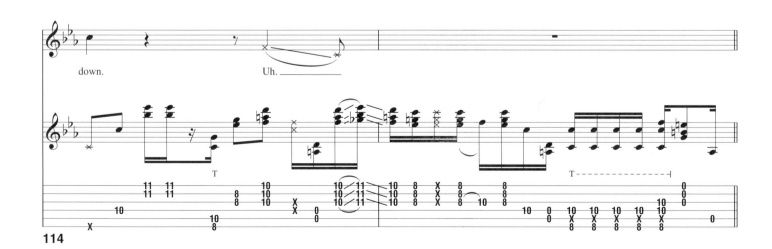

down.   Uh.

Outro

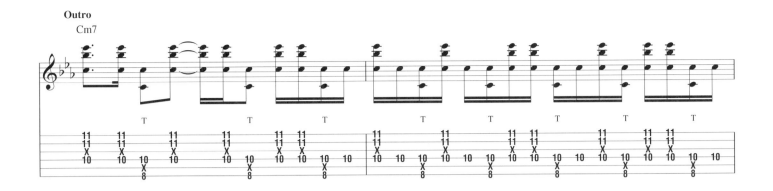

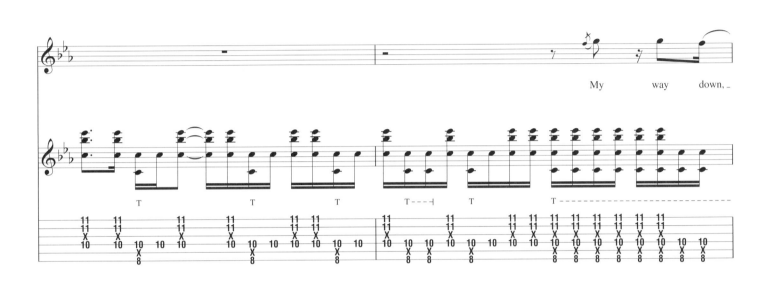

My   way   down, _

_   my   way   down. _____

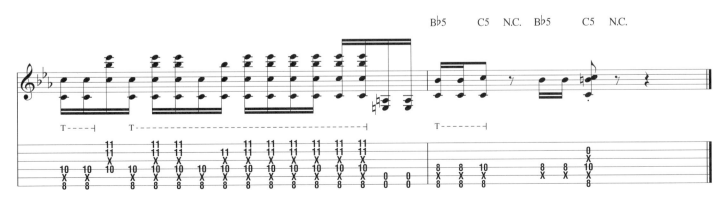

from Joe Bonamassa - *Had to Cry Today*

Never Make Your Move Too Soon

Words and Music by Will Jennings and Nesbert Hooper

*Symbols in parentheses represent chord names respective to capoed guitar.
Symbols above reflect actual sounding chords. Capoed fret is "0" in tab.

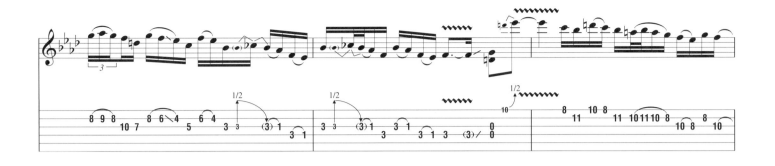

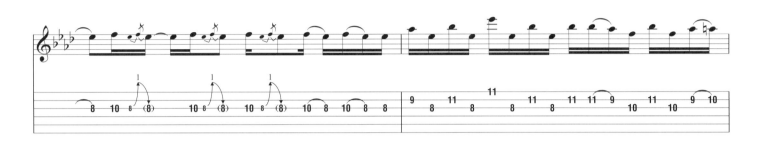

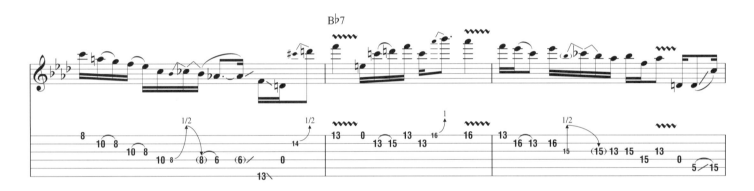

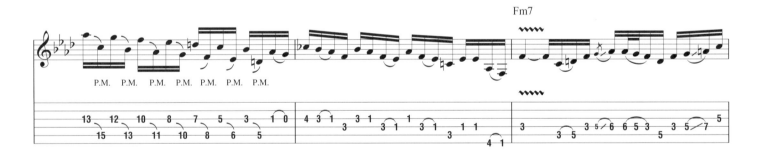

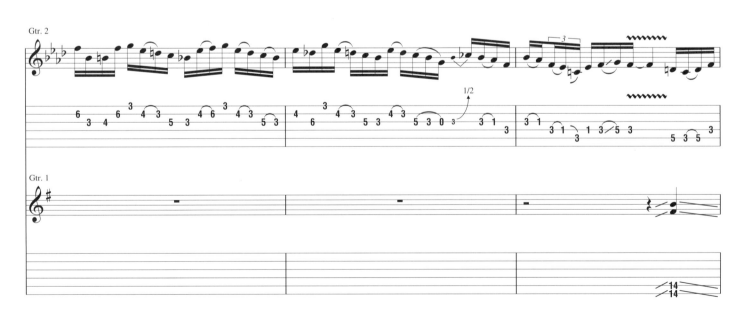

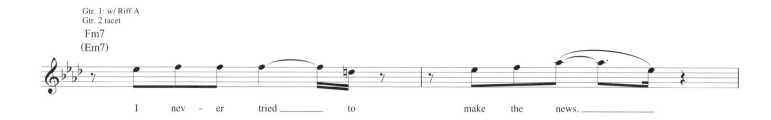

Gtr. 1: w/ Riff A
Gtr. 2 tacet

Fm7
(Em7)

I nev- er tried ____ to make the news. ____

D.S. al Coda

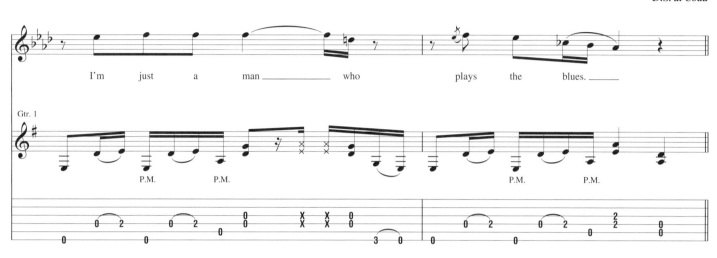

I'm just a man ____ who plays the blues. ____

Gtr. 1

P.M.   P.M.   P.M.   P.M.

Coda

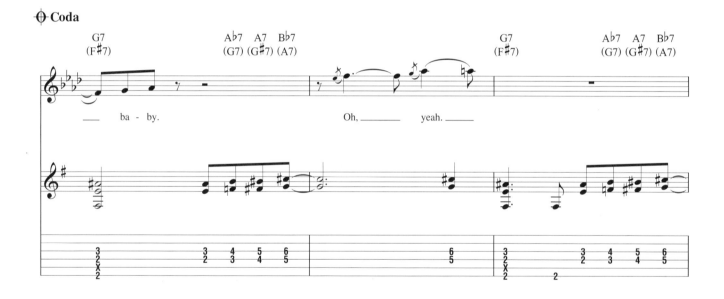

G7   A♭7 A7 B♭7   G7   A♭7 A7 B♭7
(F#7)   (G7)(G#7)(A7)   (F#7)   (G7)(G#7)(A7)

____ ba- by.   Oh, ____ yeah. ____

G7   C7
(F#7)   (B7)

Whoa, ____ yeah. ____   Oh, ____

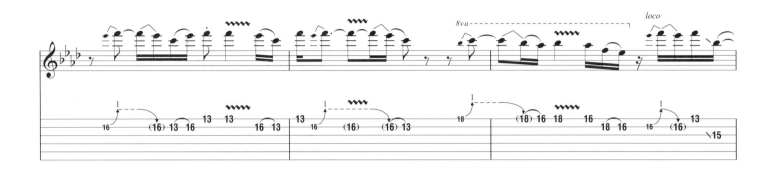

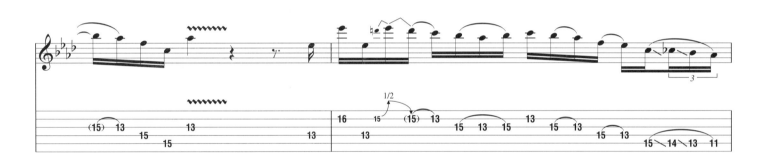

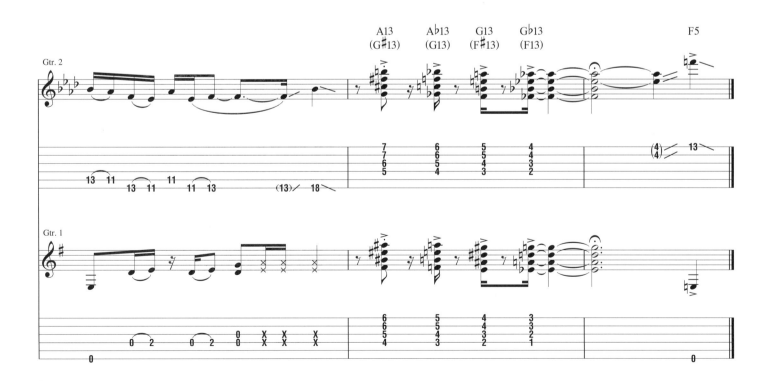

Right Next Door

By Dennis Walker

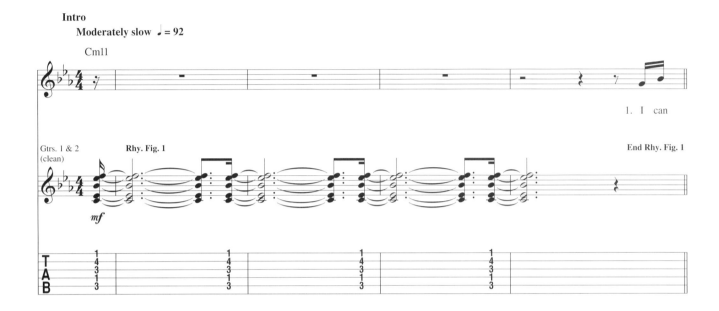

*Chord symbols reflect overall harmony.

words   sound   clear   through these   thin __ walls. ____   A - round

mid - night   I heard him   shout,   "Un - faith - ful wom - an,"   and I

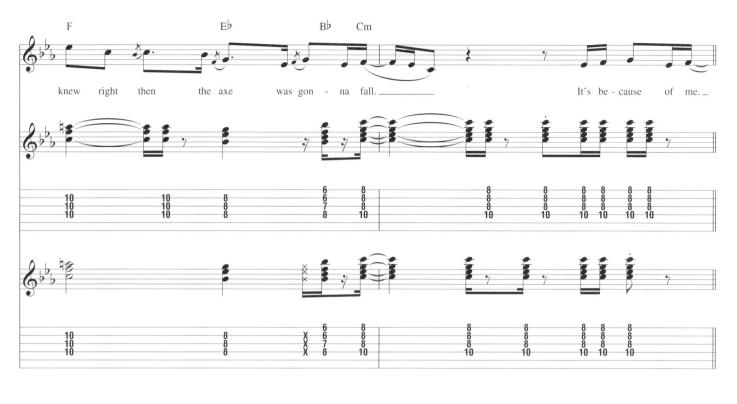

knew right then the axe was gon - na fall. _____ It's be - cause of me. __

Pre-Chorus

It's be - cause of me. __ 2. I

Gtrs. 1 & 2   **Riff A**   **End Riff A**

let ring - - - - - - - - - - - -   let ring - - - - - - - - - - - -

Verse

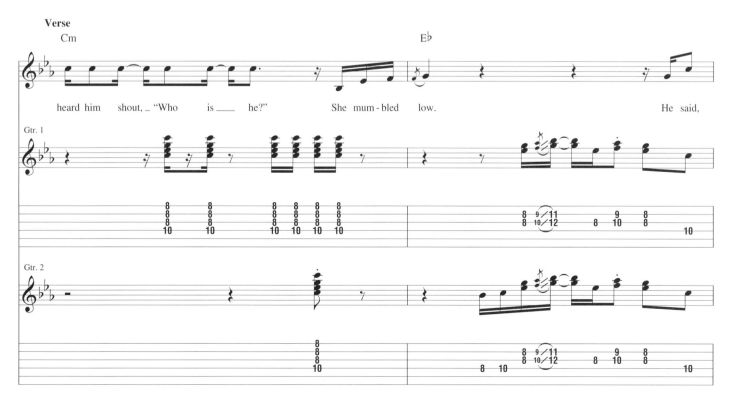

heard him shout, _ "Who is ___ he?" She mum - bled low. He said,

Gtr. 1

Gtr. 2

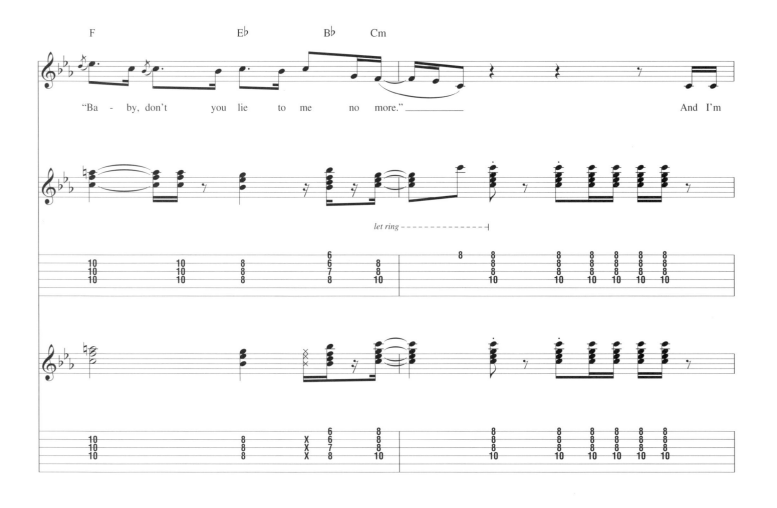

"Ba - by, don't you lie to me no more." _____ And I'm

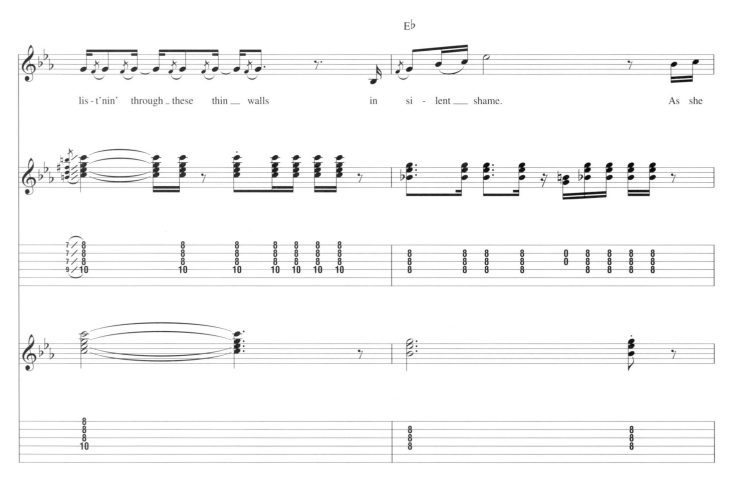

lis - t'nin' through _ these thin _ walls in si - lent _ shame. As she

called out my name,_____ I was right next door._____ It's be-cause of me.__

Pre-Chorus

Gtr. 2: w/ Riff A (2 times)

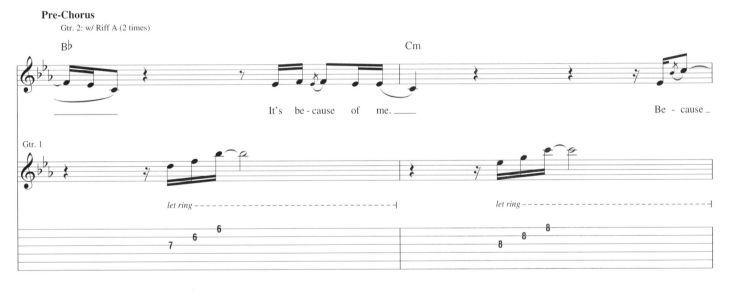

It's be-cause of me.____ Be - cause_

Gtr. 1

let ring -   let ring -

_ of me.   It's be-cause of me.___   Oh,   she was

let ring -   let ring -

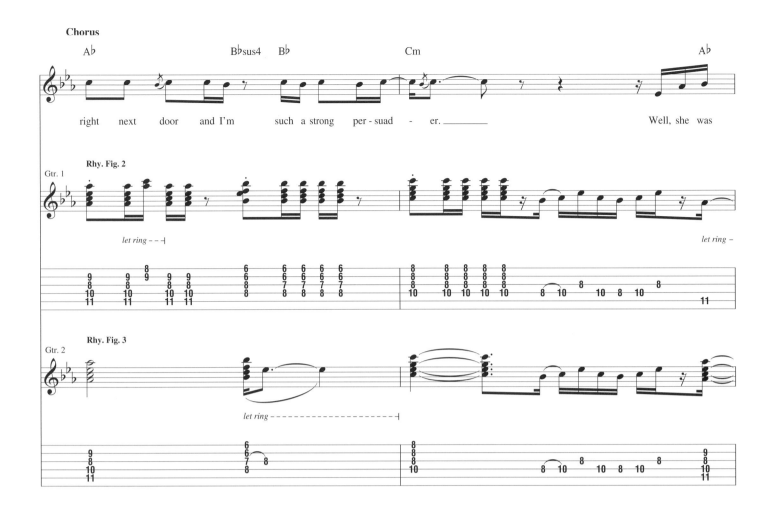

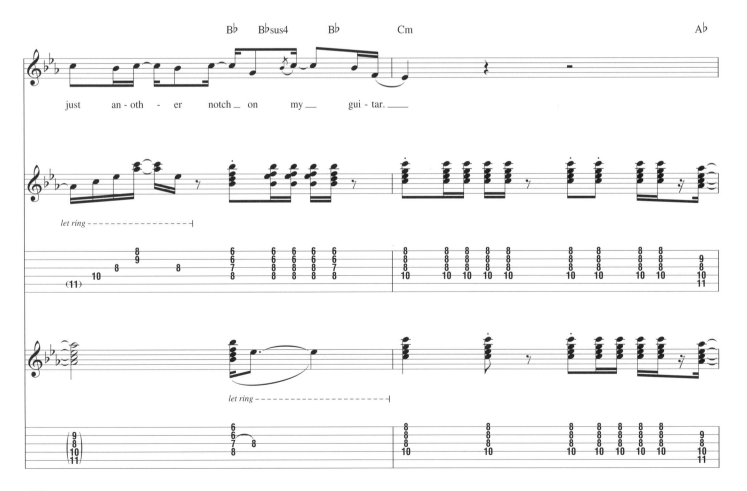

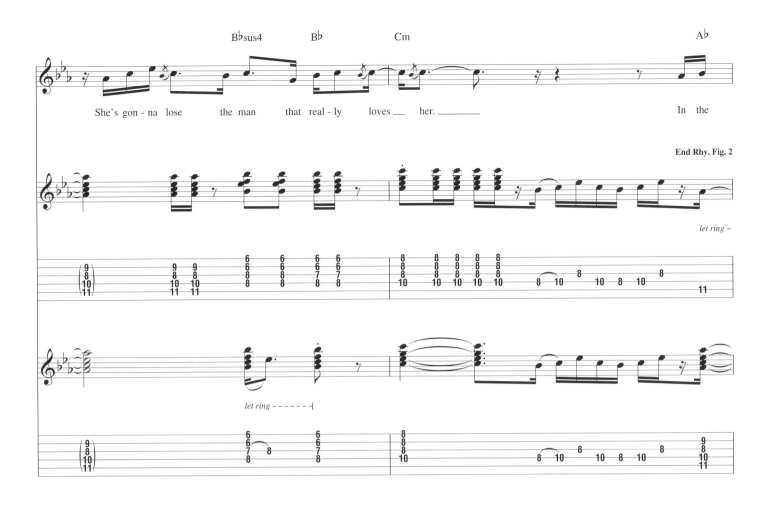

She's gon-na lose the man that real-ly loves ___ her. ___ In the

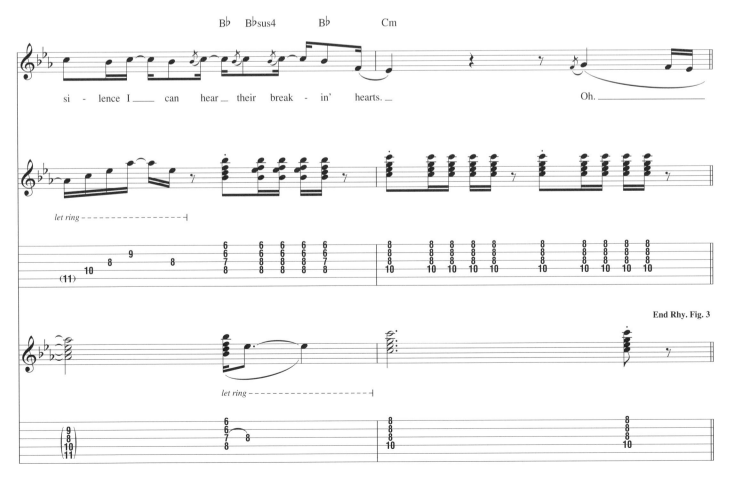

si - lence I ___ can hear ___ their break - in' hearts. ___ Oh.

Interlude

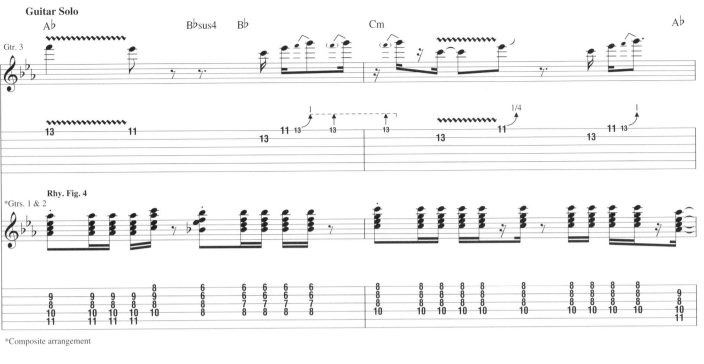

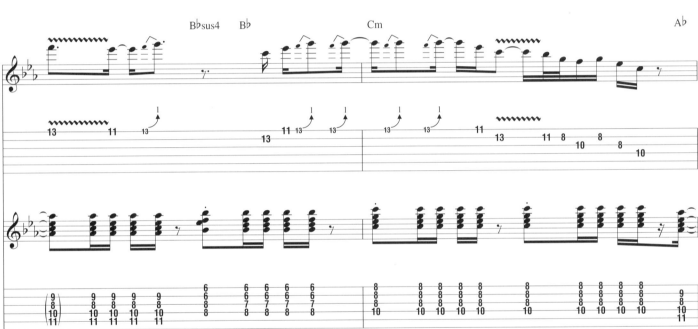

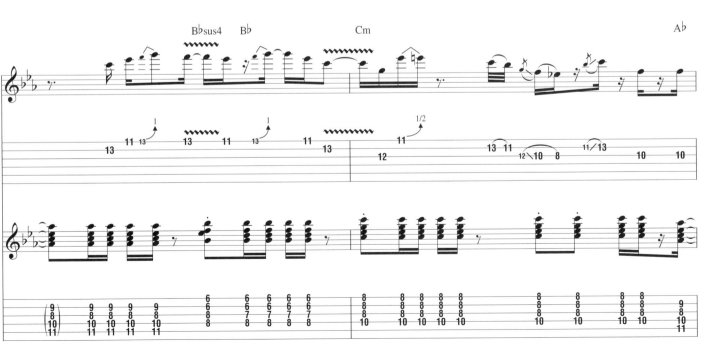

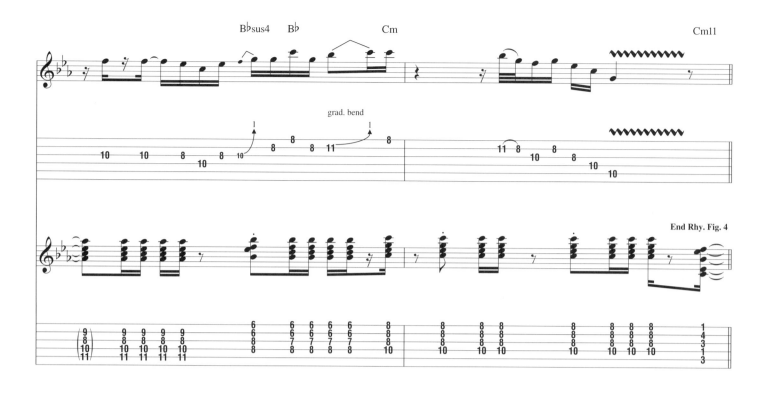

Interlude

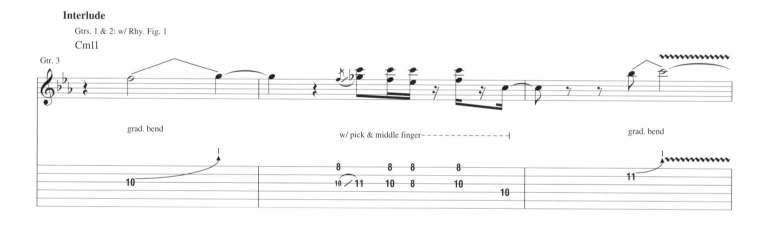

Verse

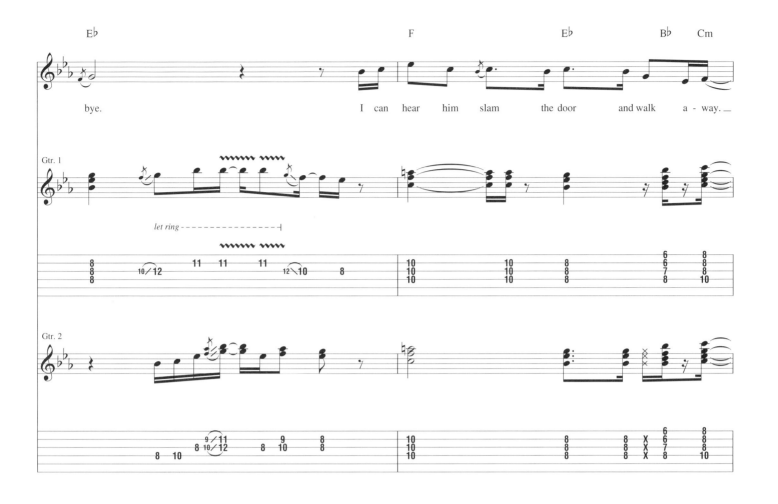

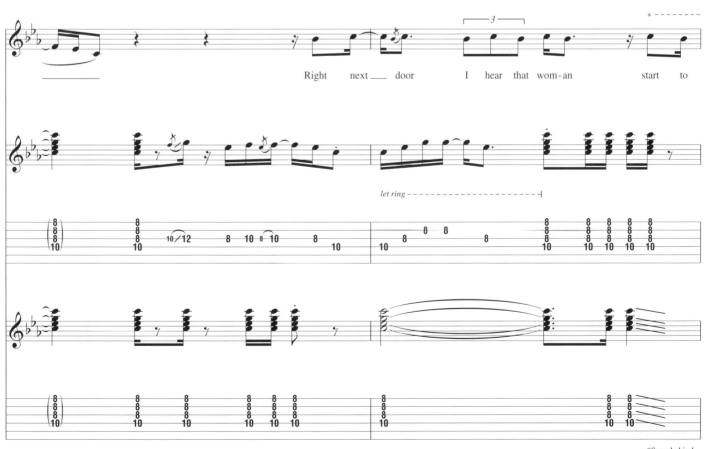

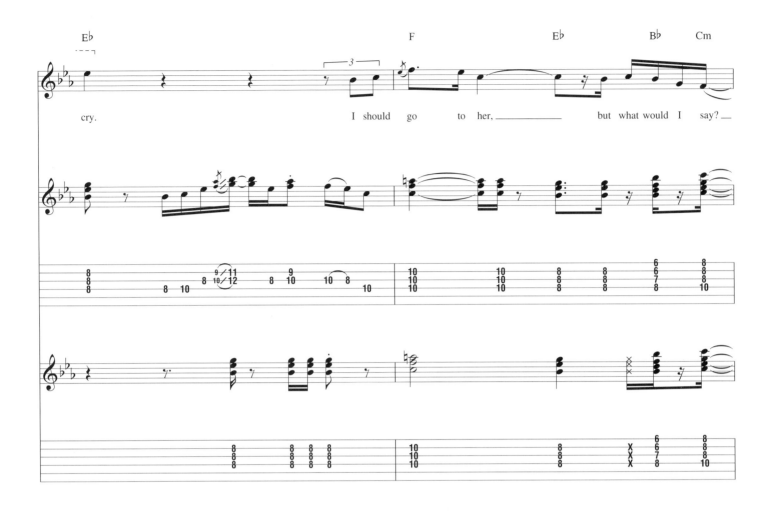

cry.   I should go to her, _____ but what would I say? ___

Pre-Chorus

Gtr. 2: w/ Riff A (2 times)

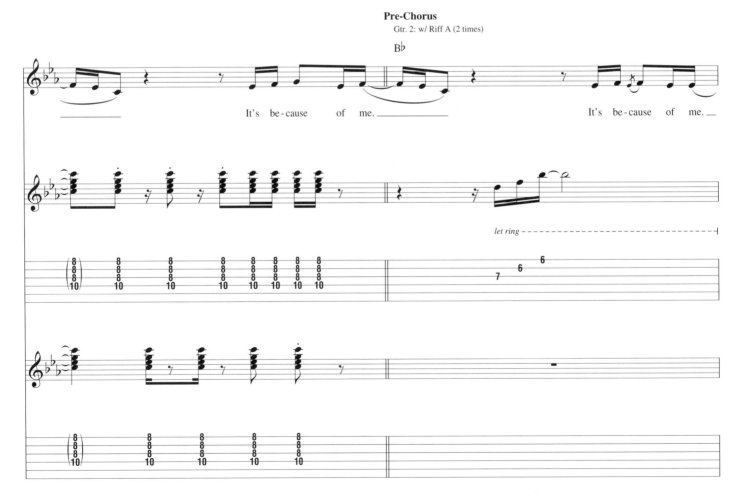

_____ It's be-cause of me. _____ It's be-cause of me. __

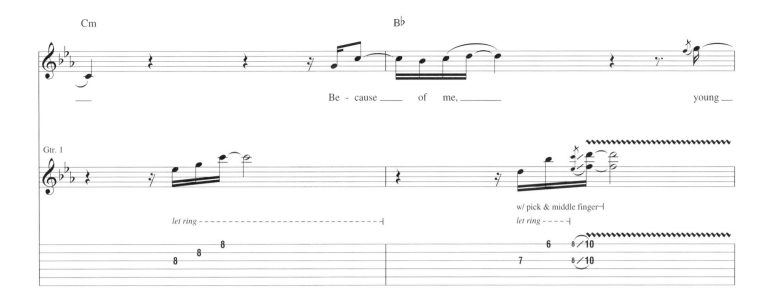

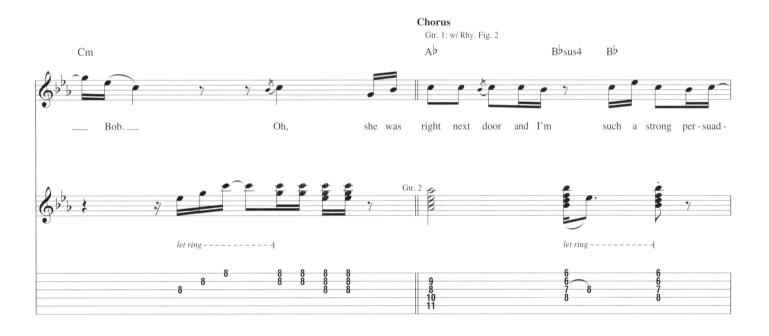

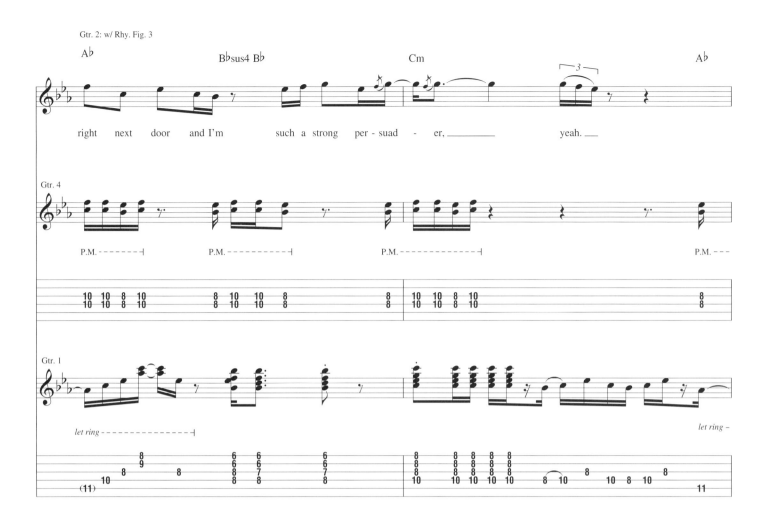

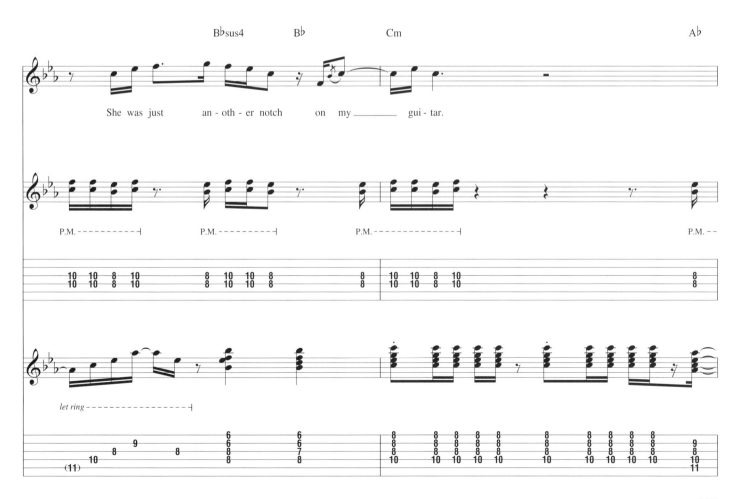

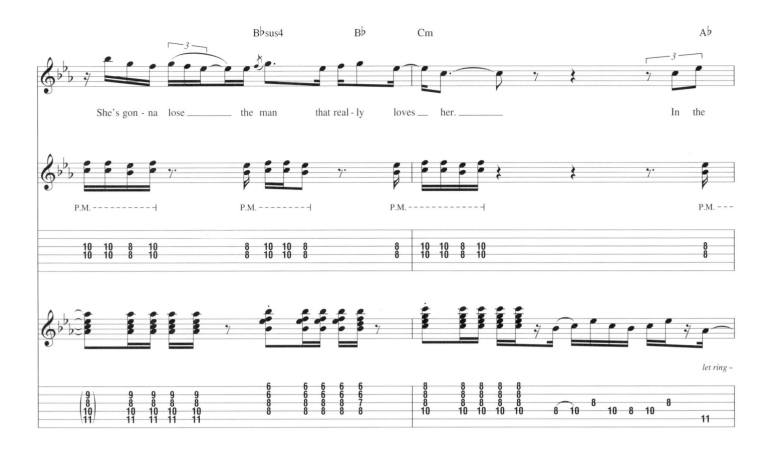

She's gon - na lose _____ the man that real - ly loves _____ her. _____ In the

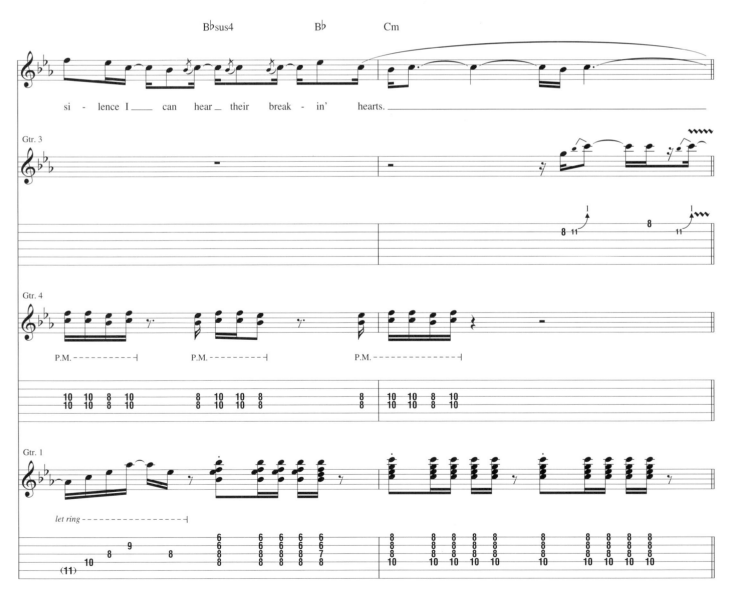

si - lence I _____ can hear _____ their break - in' hearts. _____

Guitar Solo

Gtrs. 1 & 2: w/ Rhy. Fig. 4
Gtr. 4 tacet

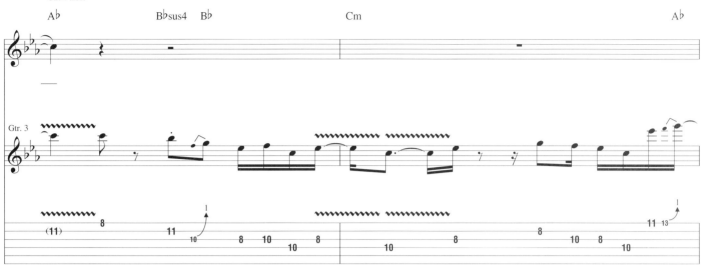

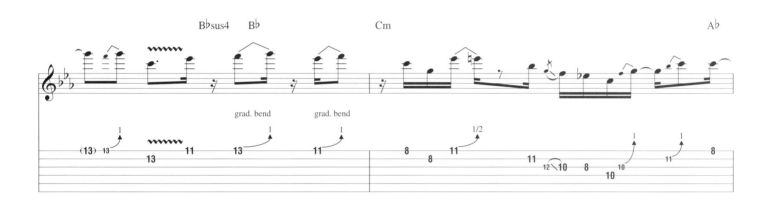

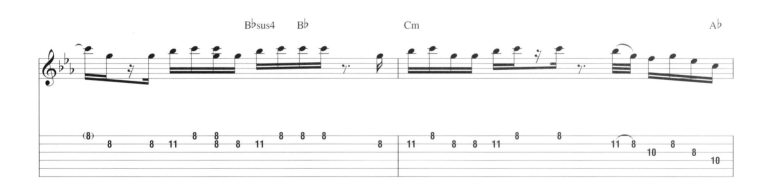

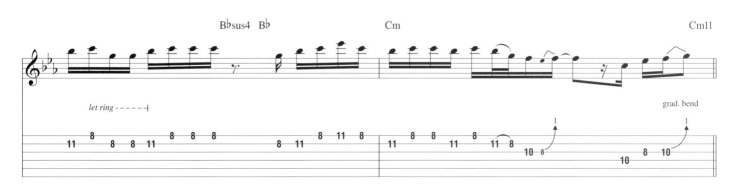

Outro

Gtrs. 1 & 2: w/ Rhy. Fig. 1 (1st 2 meas., 4 times)

Cm11

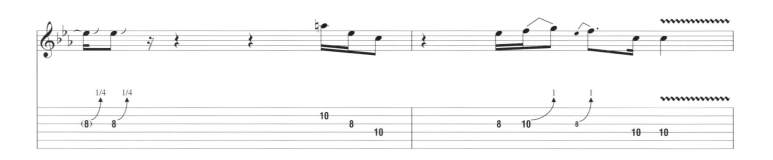

Begin fade

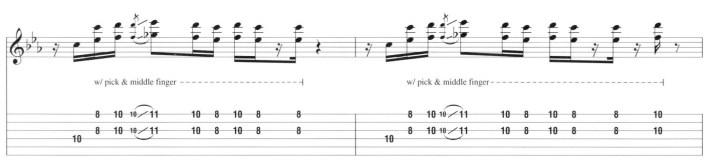

Fade out

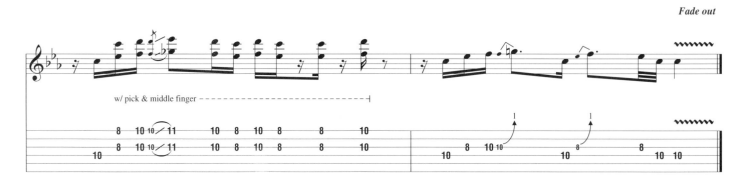

from Susan Tedeschi - *Just Won't Burn*

Rock Me Right

Words and Music by Tom Hambridge

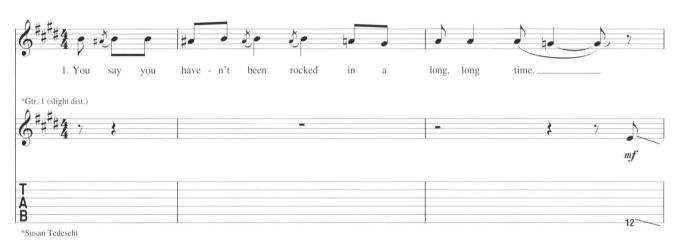

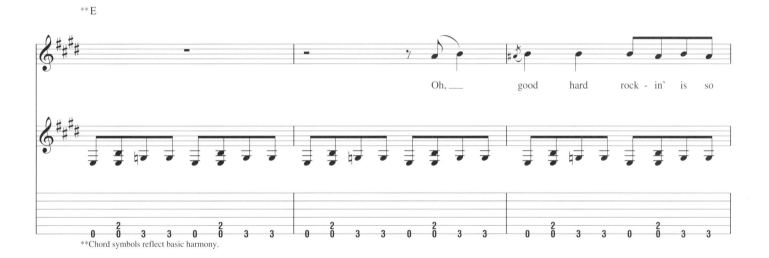

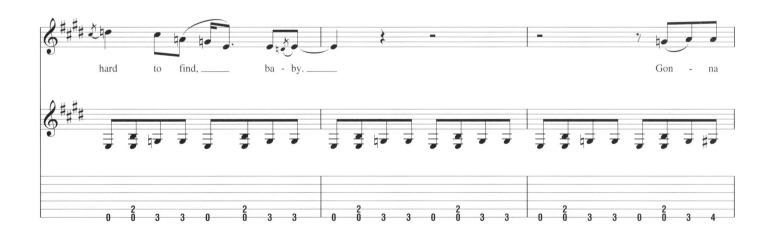

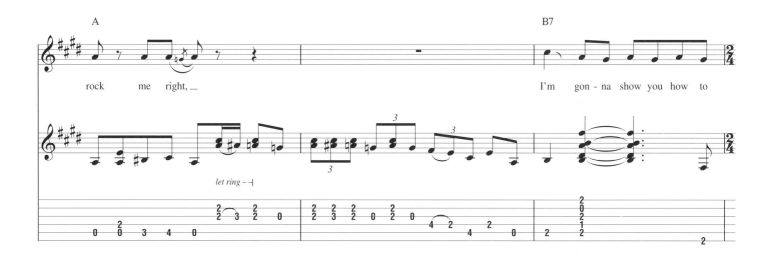

rock me right, ___ I'm gon-na show you how to

Gtr. 1: w/ Rhy. Fig. 1 (3 times)

rock me right. Rock me right

Guitar Solo

Gtr. 2 tacet

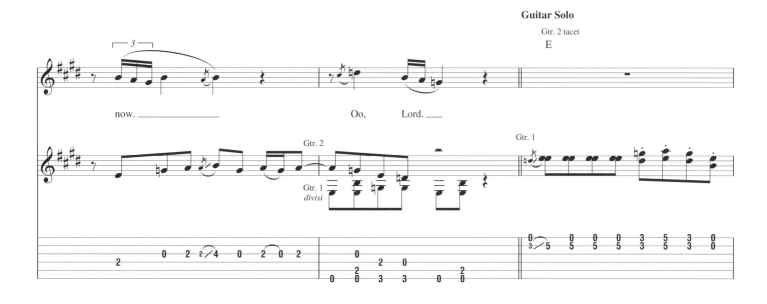

now. ___ Oo, Lord. ___

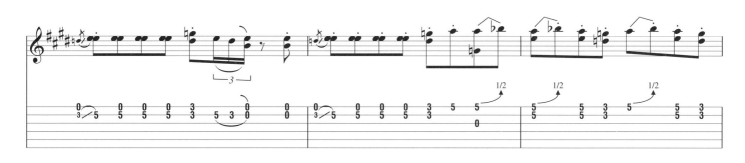

*Refers to open E string only.

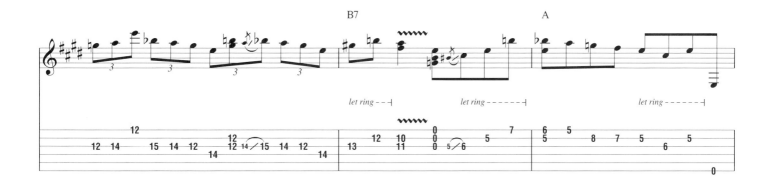

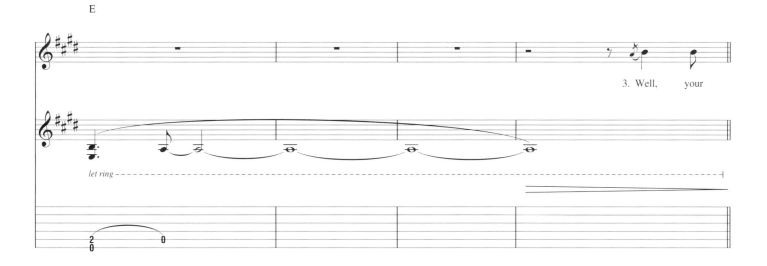

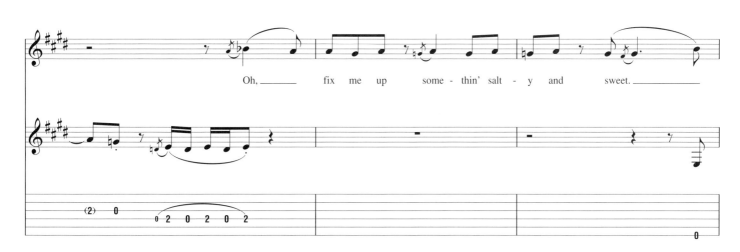

Oh, ___ c'-mon and rock me right, Lord, ___ oh, ___

rock me right now, ___ oh, ___ rock me right. ___

I'm gon-na show you how to rock me

Interlude

Gtr. 1: w/ Rhy. Fig. 1 (8 times)

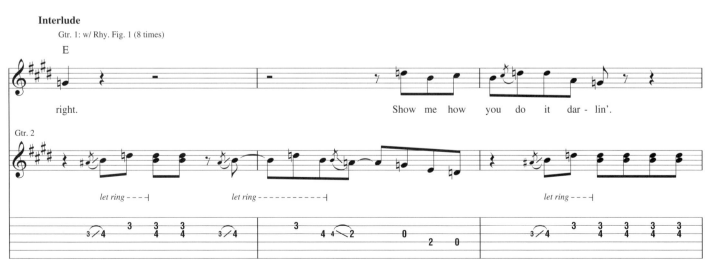

right. Show me how you do it dar-lin'.

Show ___ me how you do it ba - by. ___

Outro-Guitar Solo

Gtr. 1: w/ Rhy. Fig. 1 (till fade)

E

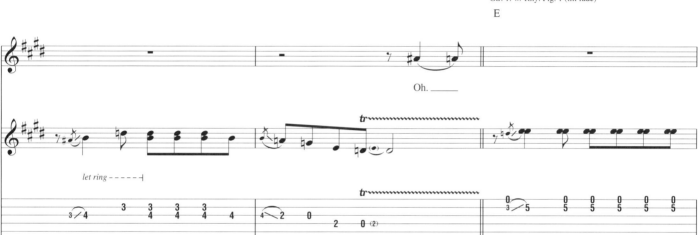

Oh. ___

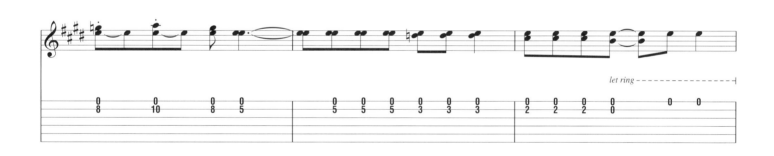

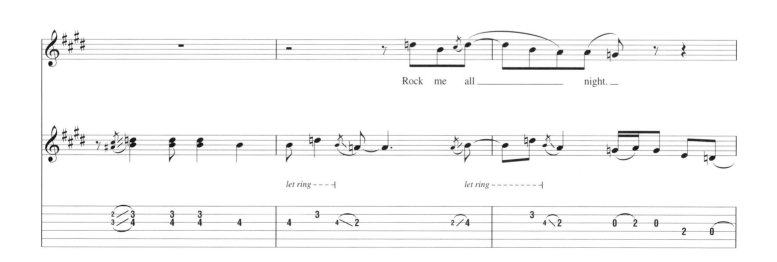

Rock me all ___ night. ___

151

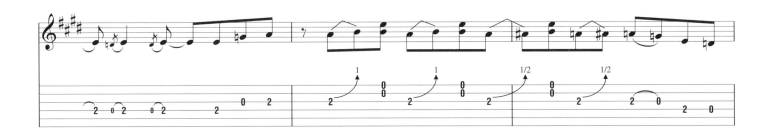

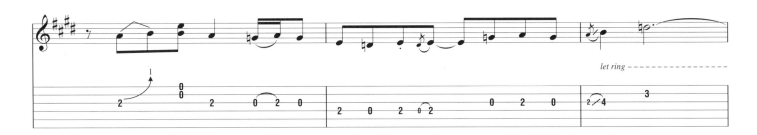

Begin fade

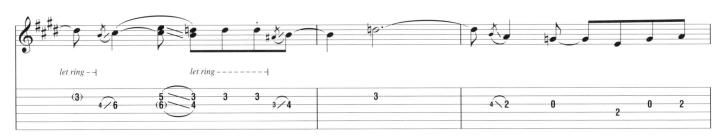

Fade out

from Robben Ford & The Blue Line - *Handful of Blues*

Rugged Road

Words and Music by Robben Ford

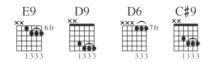

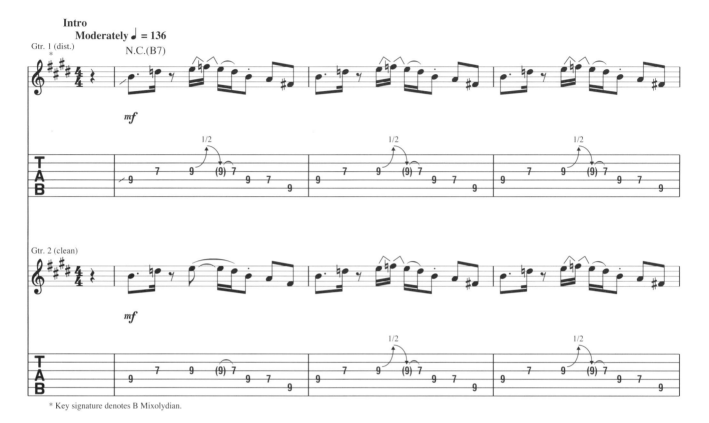

* Key signature denotes B Mixolydian.

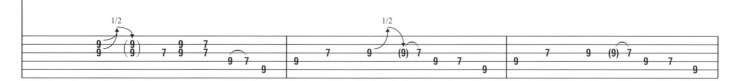

head full of trou - ble

and car-ry - in' a heav-y, heav-y load.

I was stum-bl - in' __ blind, _

com - in' down that _ rug-ged

* Sung behind the beat.

road.   Yeah, and no ____ one could help ____ me.

I had to walk that road   a - lone.

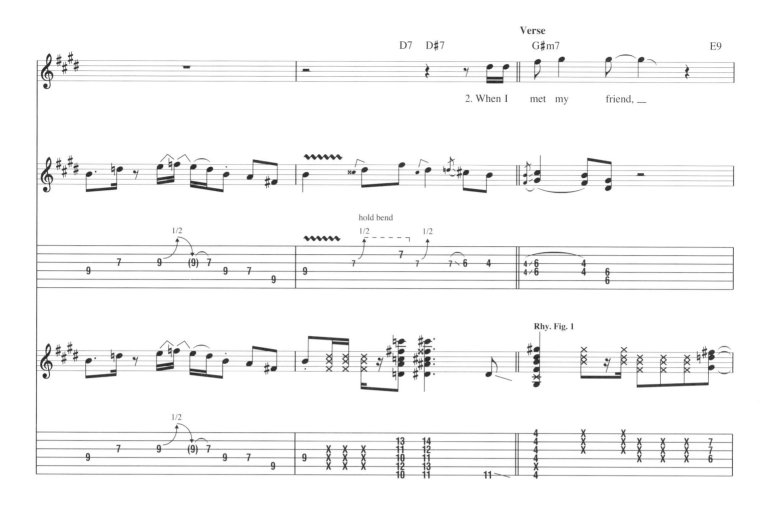

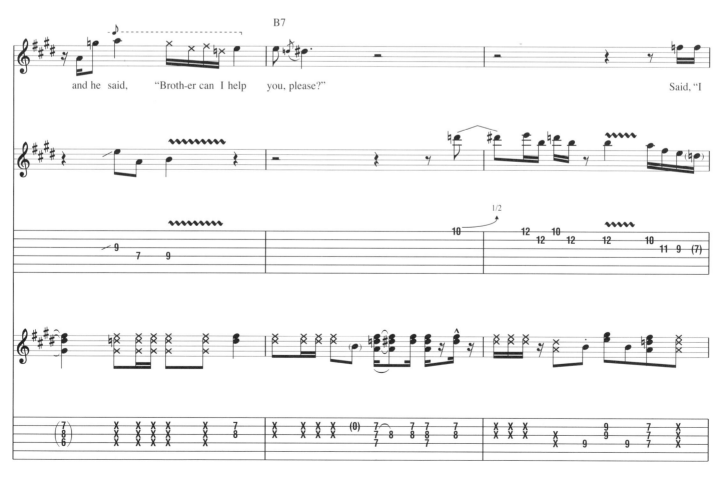

know you've got some wor-ries, may-be some that I can ease."

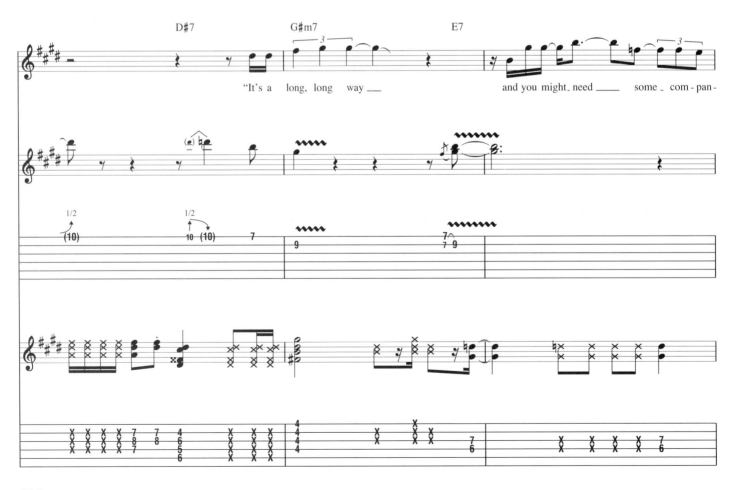

"It's a long, long way ___ and you might ___ need ___ some _ com-pan-

Interlude

Guitar Solo

N.C.(D7)

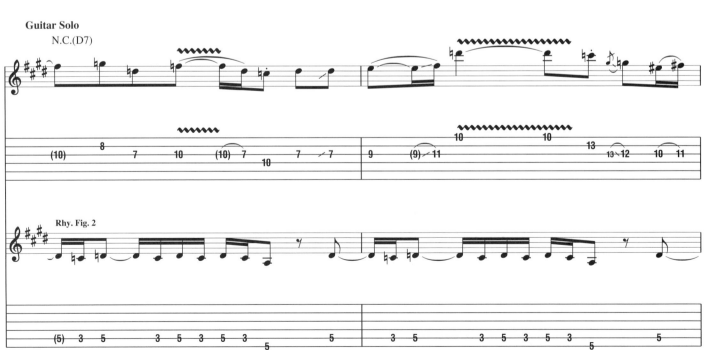

Rhy. Fig. 2

my   life   has   just   be - gun. __

Guitar Solo
Gtr. 2: w/ Rhy. Fig. 2
(D7)
Gtr. 1

(B7)

* Played behind the beat.

Outro

N.C.(B7)

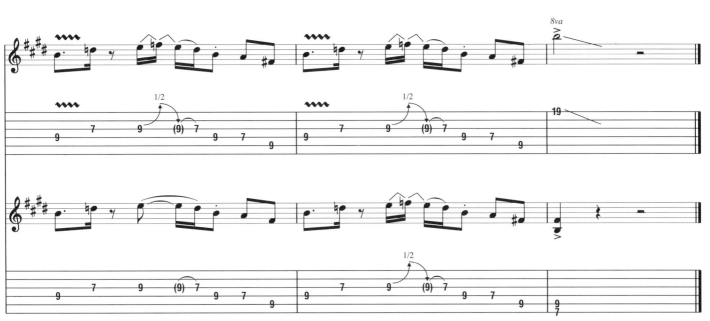

She's Into Something

Words and Music by Carl Wright

Gtr. 3: Open Dm tuning, capo V:
(low to high) D-A-D-F-A-D

†Albert Collins

††Symbols in parentheses represent chord names respective to capoed Gtr. 3.
Symbols above represent actual sounding chords. Capoed fret is "0" in tab.
Chord symbols reflect basic harmony.

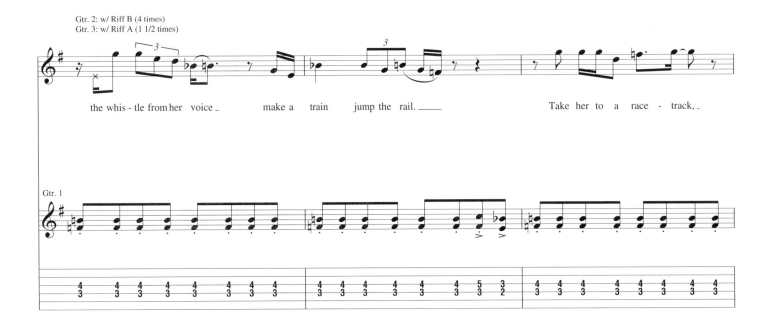

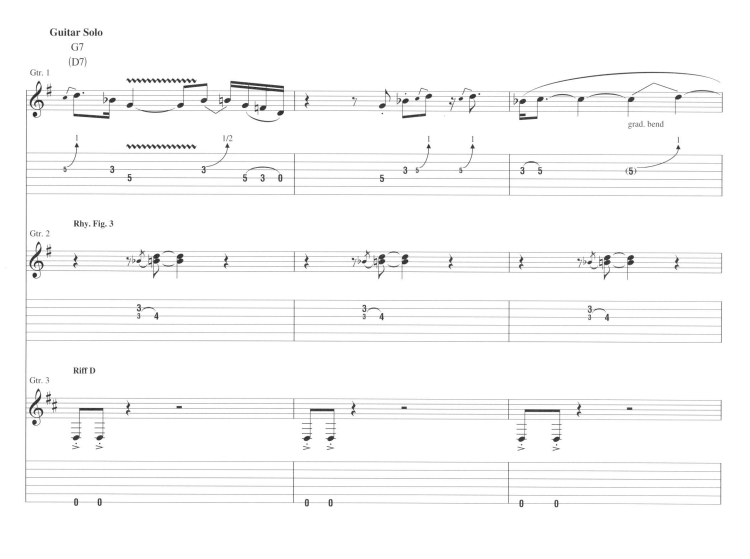

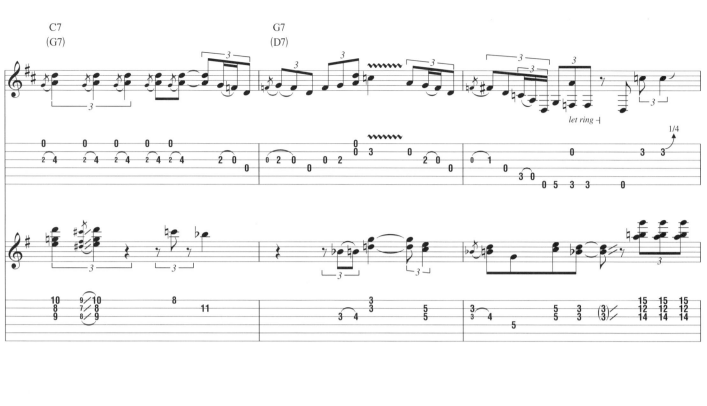

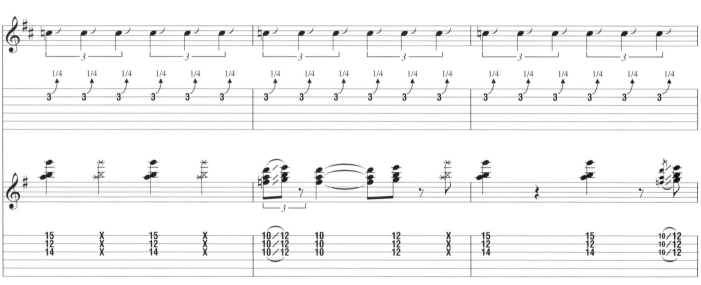

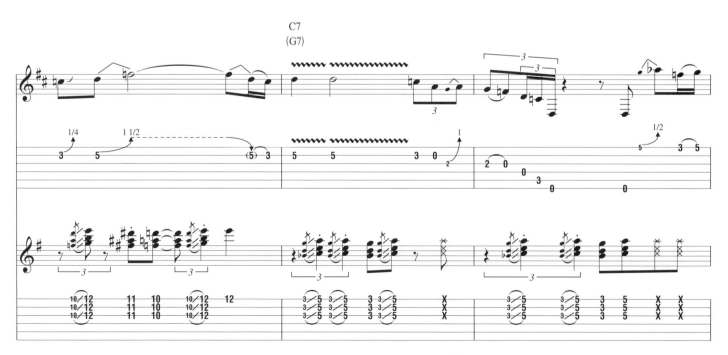

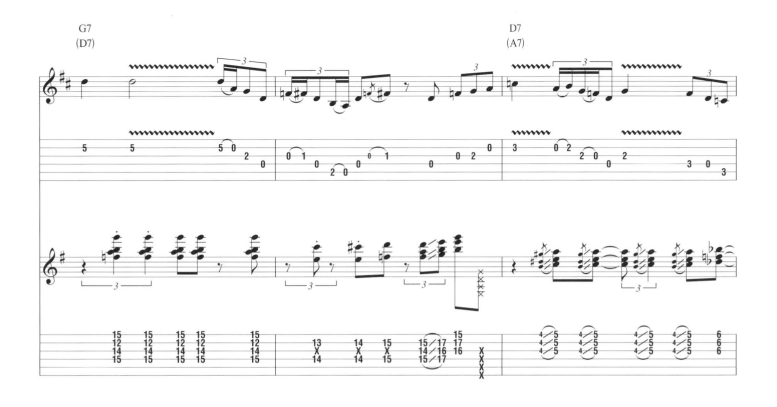

Yeah, _ yeah, __ yeah. ___

Say what she do!

Somehow, Somewhere, Someway

Words and Music by Kenny Wayne Shepherd and Danny Tate

* Chord symbols reflect overall tonality.

Verse

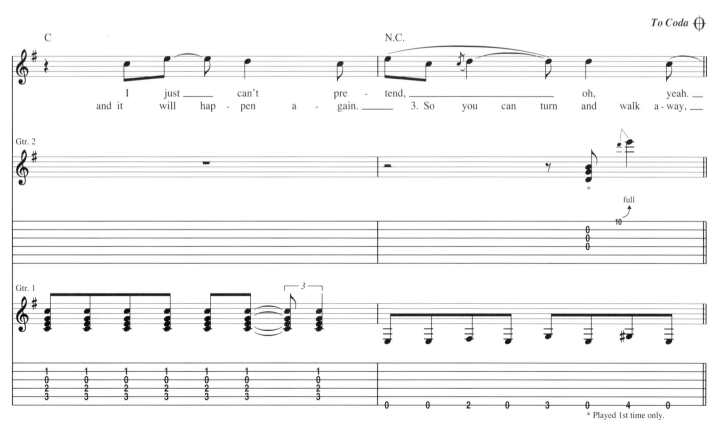

Guitar Solo

Gtr. 1: w/ Rhy. Fig. 1, 2 times, simile

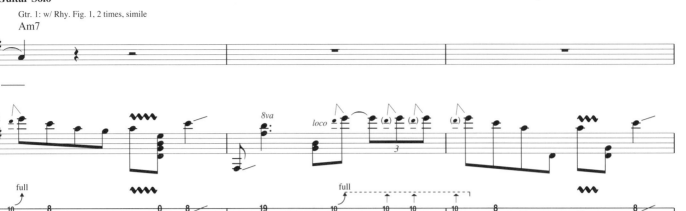

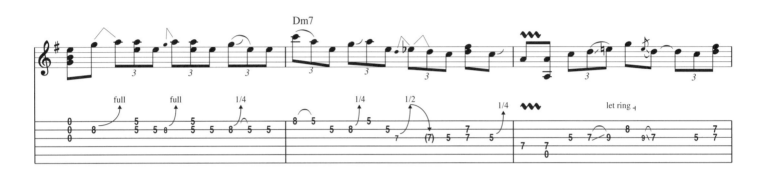

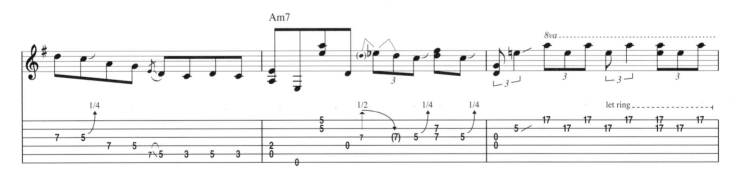

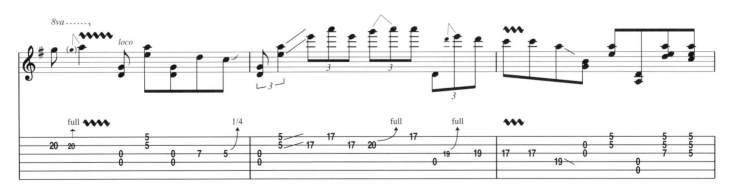

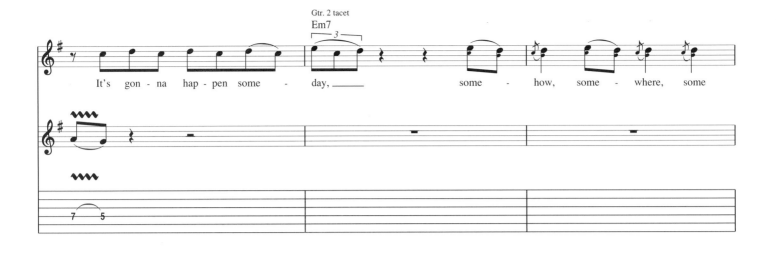

It's gon-na hap-pen some — day, _____ some - how, some - where, some

way. _ I wan-na have you some - day, _____ some -

how, some - where, some - way. _ I'll make _ you mine some - day, _____ some -

how, some - where, some - way. _ Oo, yeah. _____

Outro-Guitar Solo

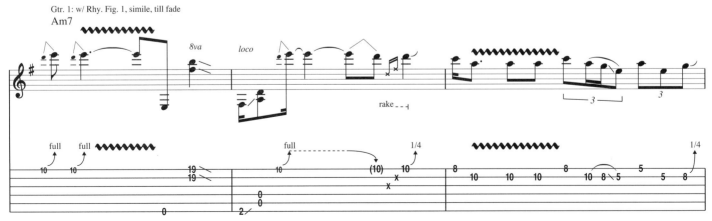

*Played behind the beat.

from The Derek Trucks Band - *Already Free*

Sweet Inspiration

Words and Music by Dan Penn and Spooner Oldham

Open E tuning:
(low to high) E-B-E-G♯-B-E

Intro
Moderately ♩ = 116

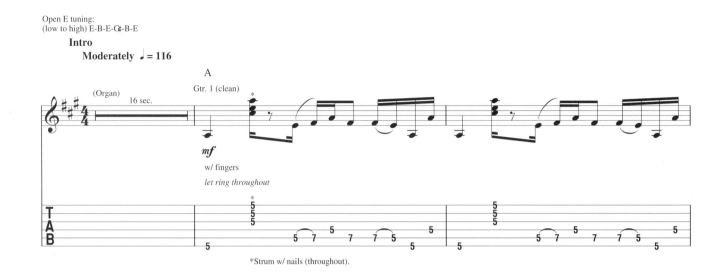

*Strum w/ nails (throughout).

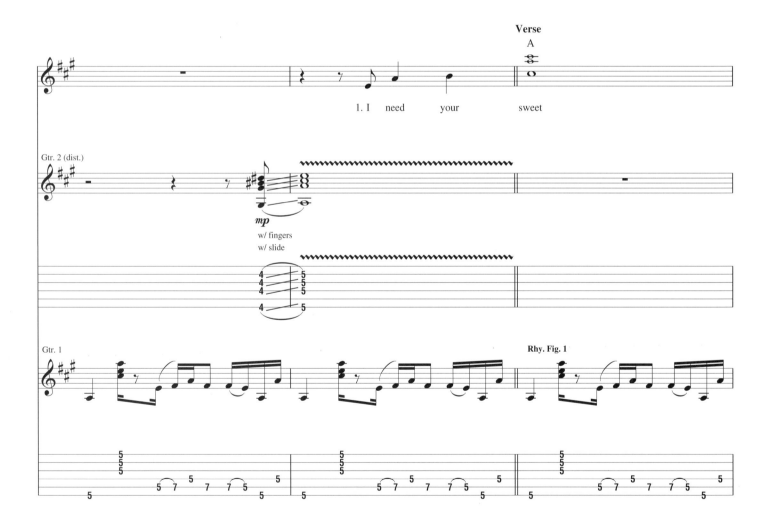

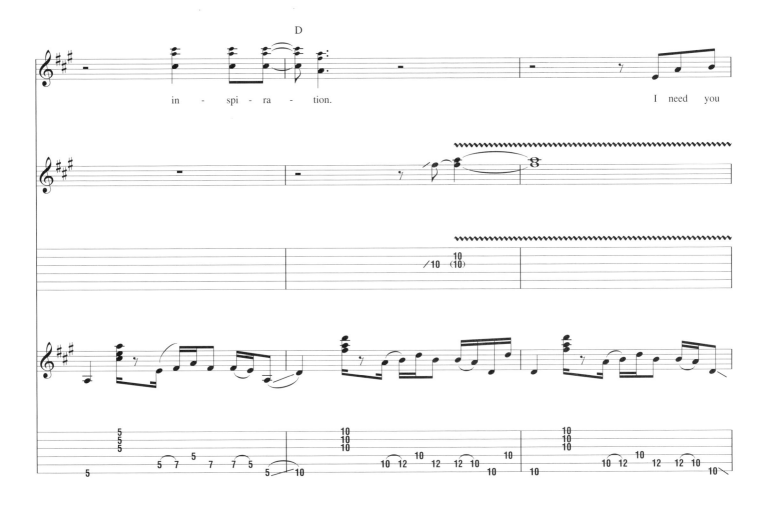

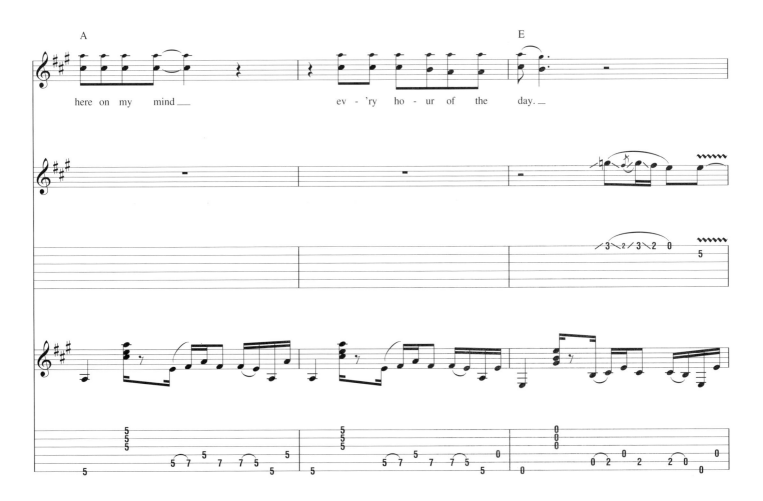

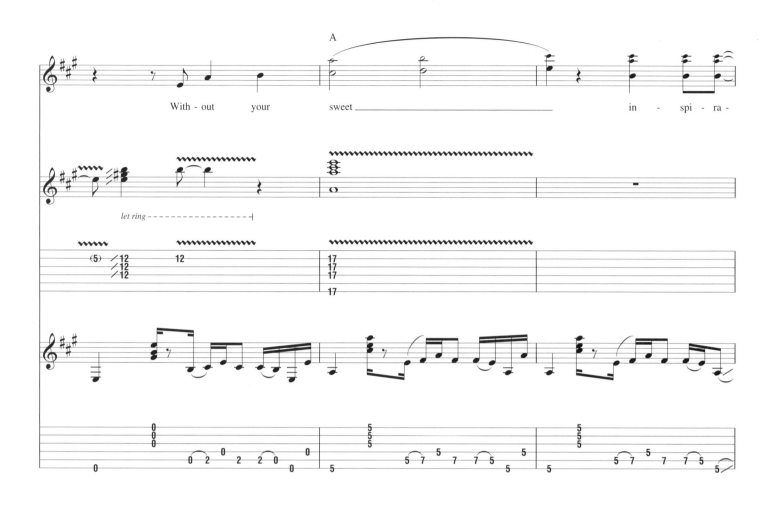

With - out   your   sweet _____   in - spi - ra -

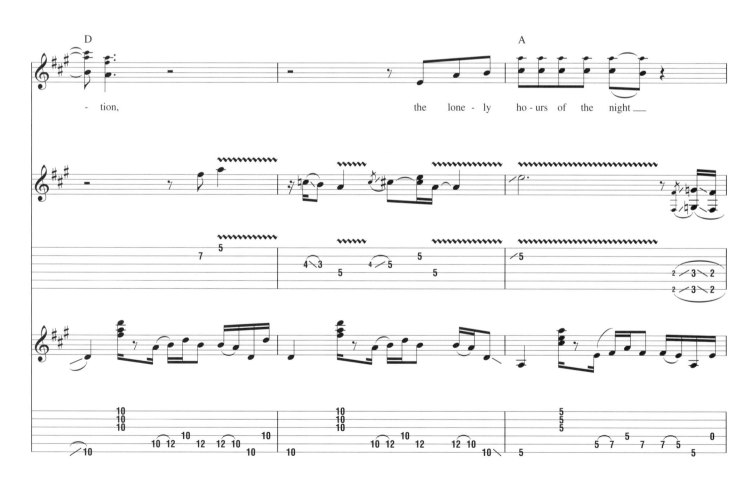

- tion,   the   lone - ly   ho - urs   of   the   night ___

193

*Dig into fretboard w/ slide.

Bridge

Gtr. 1: w/ Rhy. Fig. 2

And if I'm out in the rain, _____ ba - by, in a bad sit - u - a -
(Sweet, sweet. Sweet, sweet.

Outro

Gtr. 1: w/ Rhy. Fig. 1 (1st meas., till end)

198

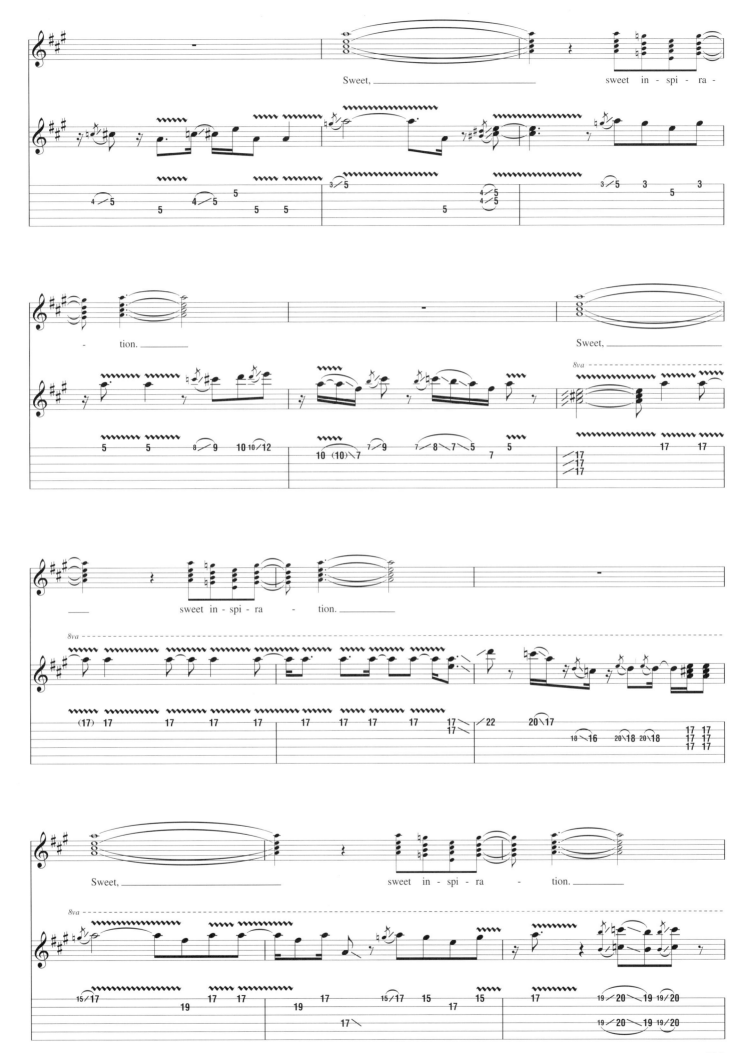

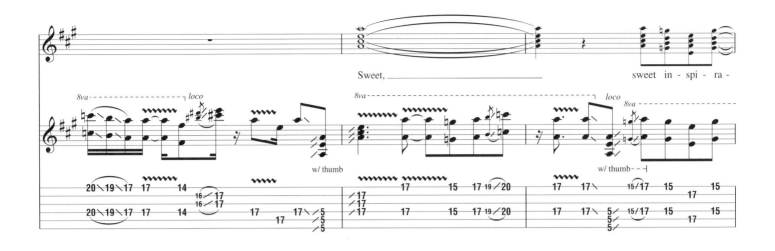

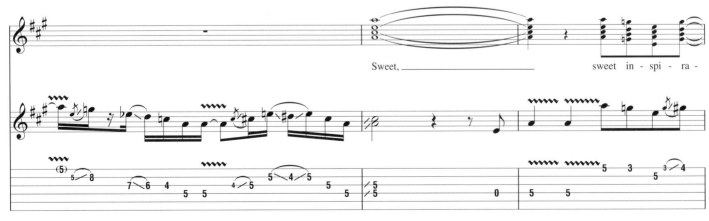

Texas Cadillac

Words and Music by Joseph Kubek and Ronald Levy

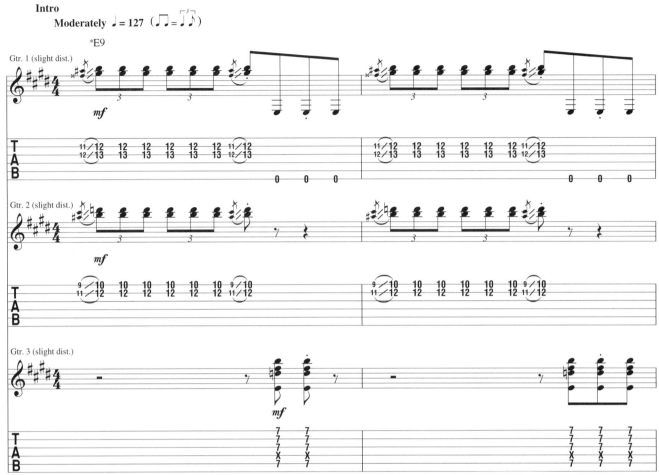

*Chord symbols reflect combined harmony.

*Chord symbols reflect basic harmony.

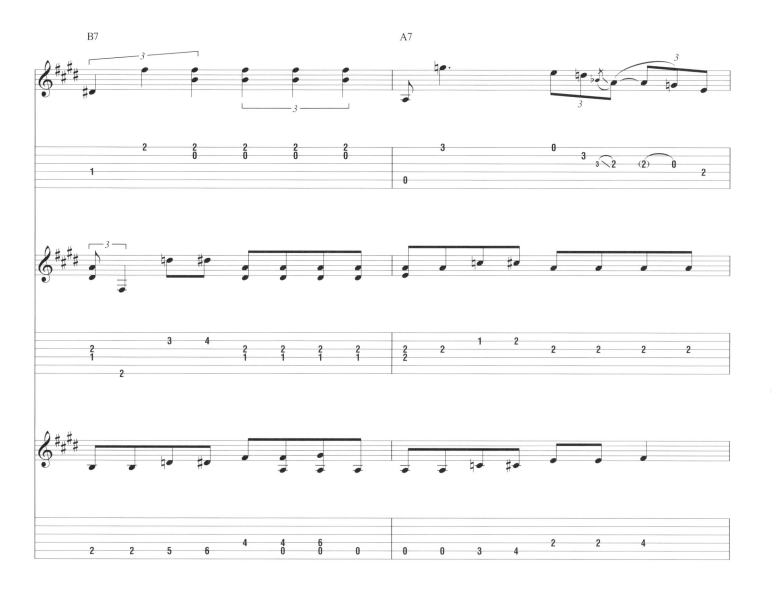

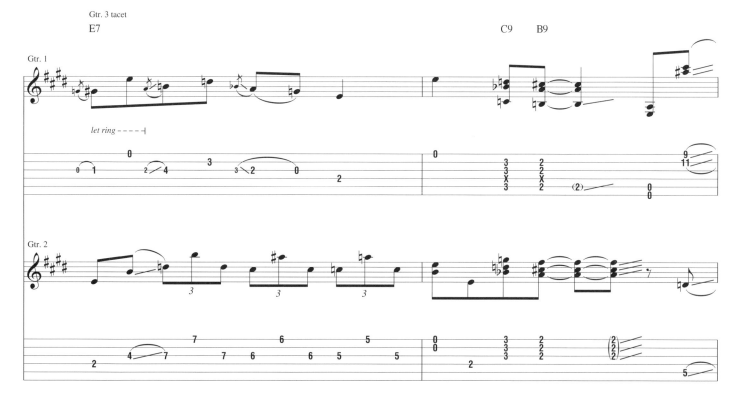

Gtr. 3: w/ Rhy. Fig. 1

Gtr. 2: w/ Rhy. Fig. 2

Gtr. 1

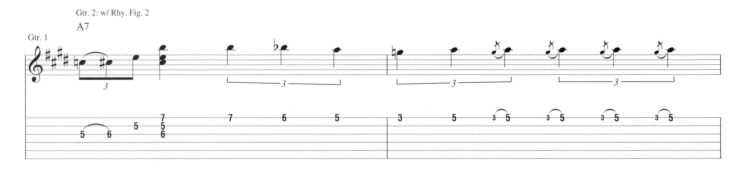

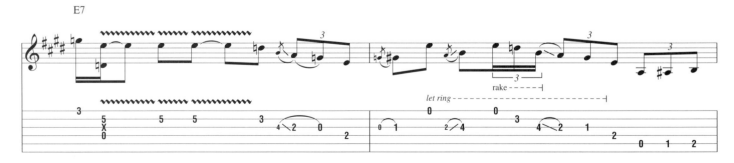

Verse

1. She's got long legs for days, sweet lips for night.

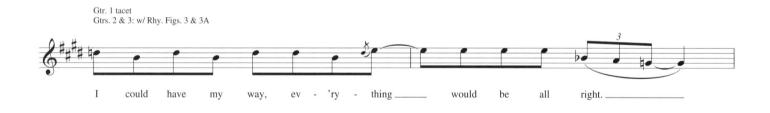

Lord, if

I could have my way, ev - 'ry - thing _____ would be all right. _____

I _____

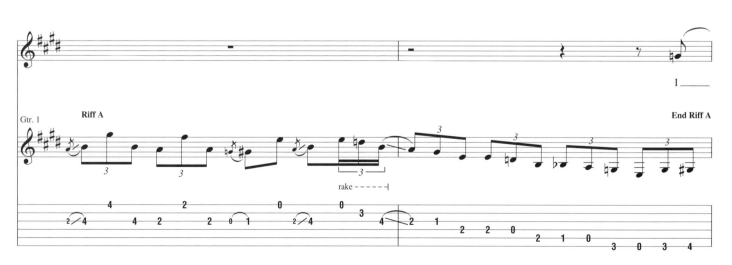

Gtr. 1 tacet
Gtrs. 2 & 3: w/ Rhy. Figs. 3 & 3A

Gtr. 1

Riff A

End Riff A

rake - - - - - ┤

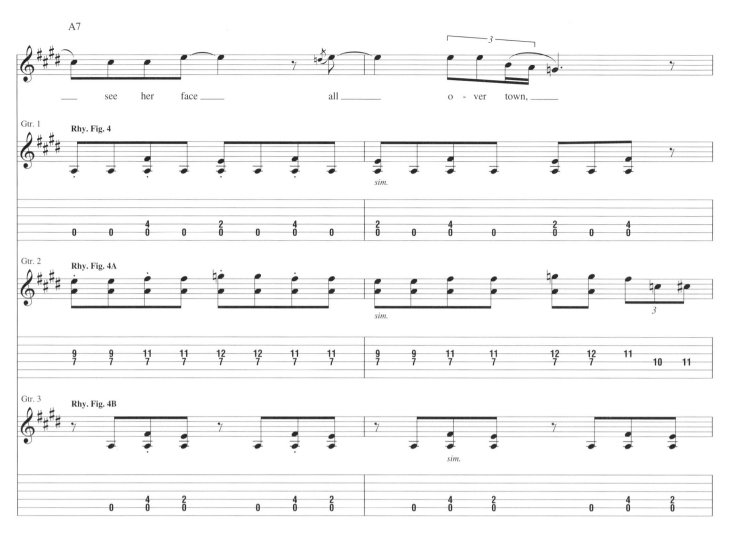

see her face ____ all ____ o - ver town, ____

in ev - 'ry place twist - in' heads a - round. ____ Oo, ee. ____

2. Now, she's

Gtrs. 2 & 3: w/ Rhy. Figs. 3 & 3A (2 times)

E7

nev - er in a hur - ry, but she's al - ways mov - in' fast. ___
may - be some night she'll come hear me sing. ___

Gtr. 1

*Sung behind the beat.

She will nev - er have to wor - ry 'cause her beau - ty will last. ___
Oh, and give me a ride ___ in a long ___ lim - ou - sine. ___

Gtr. 1: w/ Riff A

Gtrs. 1, 2 & 3: w/ Rhy. Figs. 4, 4A & 4B

A7

I ___ see her face ___ all ___

___ o - ver town, ___ in ev - 'ry place twist - in' heads a - round. ___ Oo, ee. ___

Gtr. 1: w/ Riff B
Gtrs. 2 & 3: w/ Rhy. Figs. 3 & 3A

E7

___ Oo, ee. ___ Oo, ee. ___

Gtrs. 1 & 3: w/ Rhy. Fig. 5
Gtr. 2: w/ Rhy. Fig. 5A

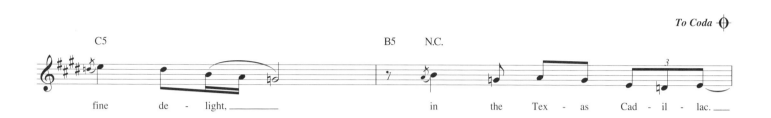

I'd like to share my wine right here from my sack, _____ with the

To Coda ⊕

fine de - light, _____ in the Tex - as Cad - il - lac. _____

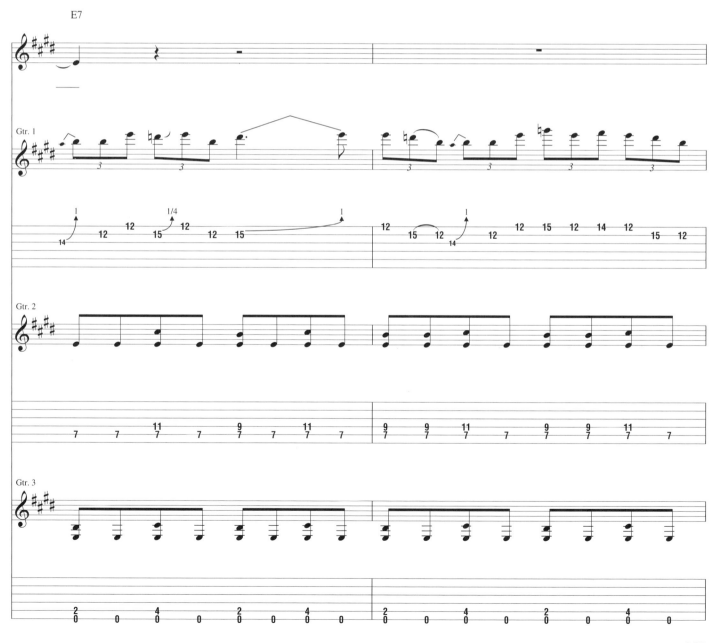

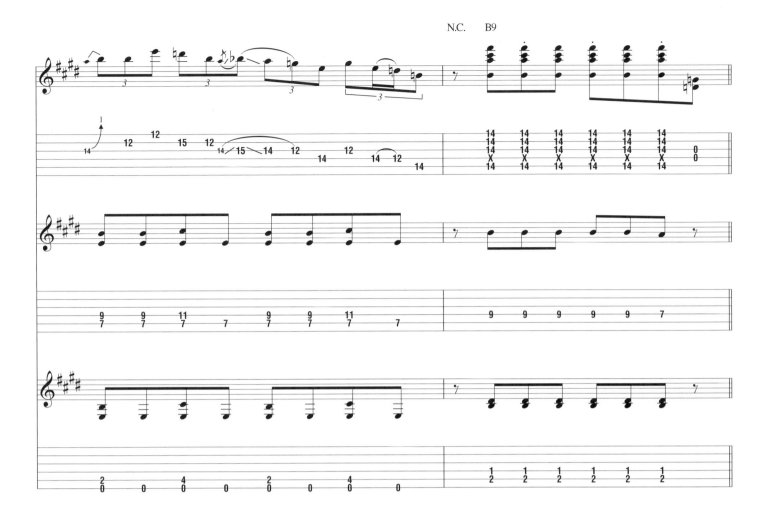

Interlude

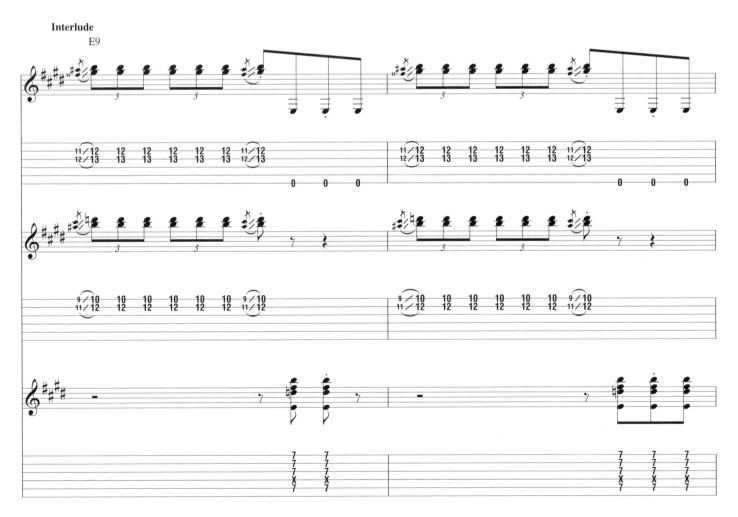

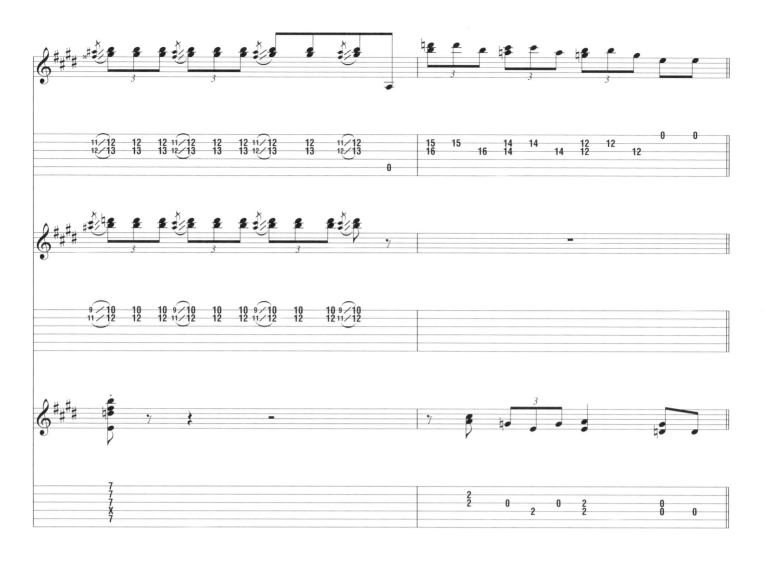

Guitar Solo

Gtr. 2: w/ Rhy. Fig. 2
Gtr. 3: w/ Rhy. Fig. 1 (last 4 meas.)

A7

Gtr. 1

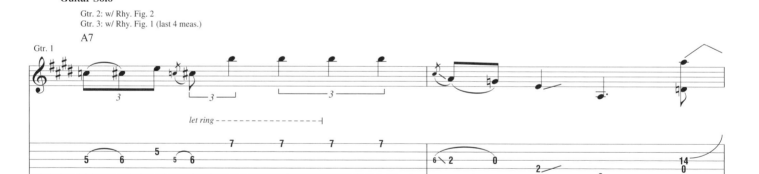

E7

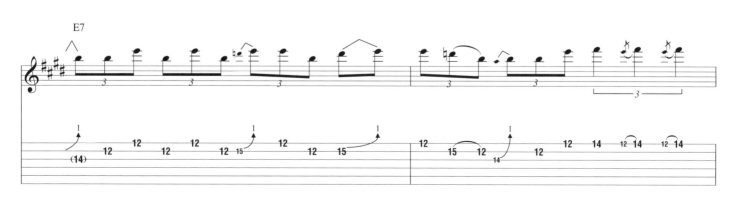

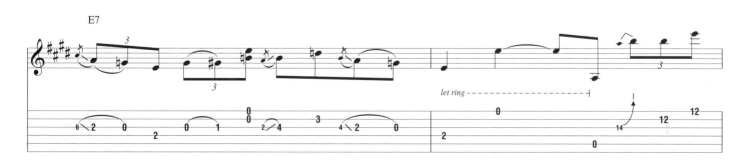

217

Gtrs. 2 & 3: w/ Riffs C & C1

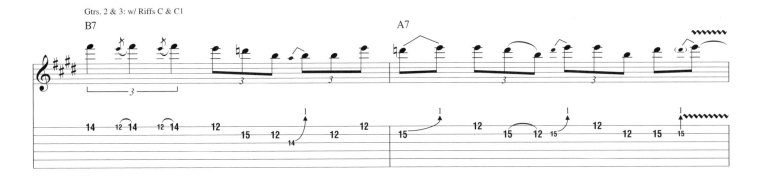

D.S. al Coda

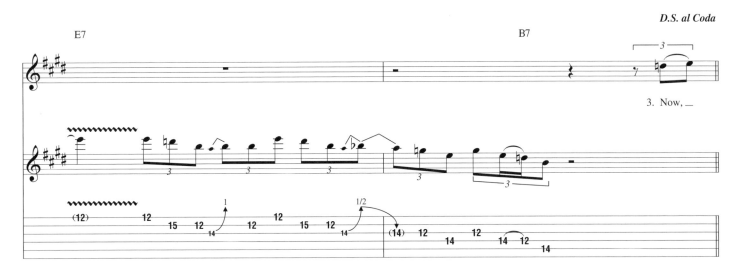

3. Now, __

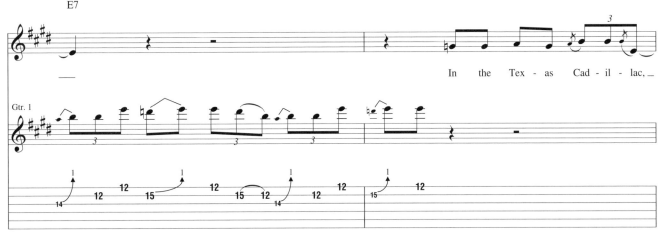

Coda

Gtr. 2: w/ Rhy. Fig. 6 (1 1/2 times)
Gtr. 3: w/ Rhy. Fig. 3A (1 1/2 times)

In the Tex - as Cad - il - lac, __

Gtr. 1

in her Tex - as Cad - il - lac, __

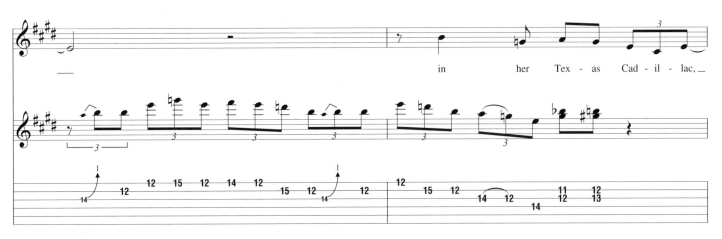

218

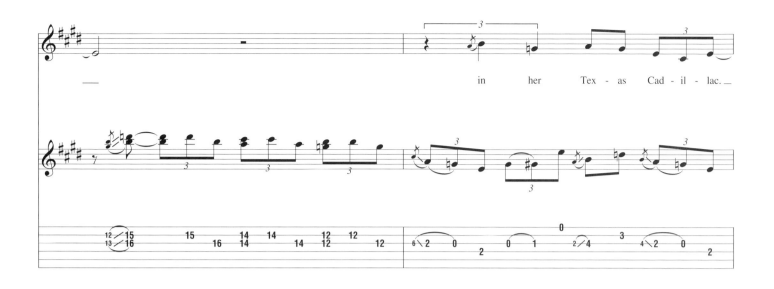

in her Tex - as Cad - il - lac.

Free time

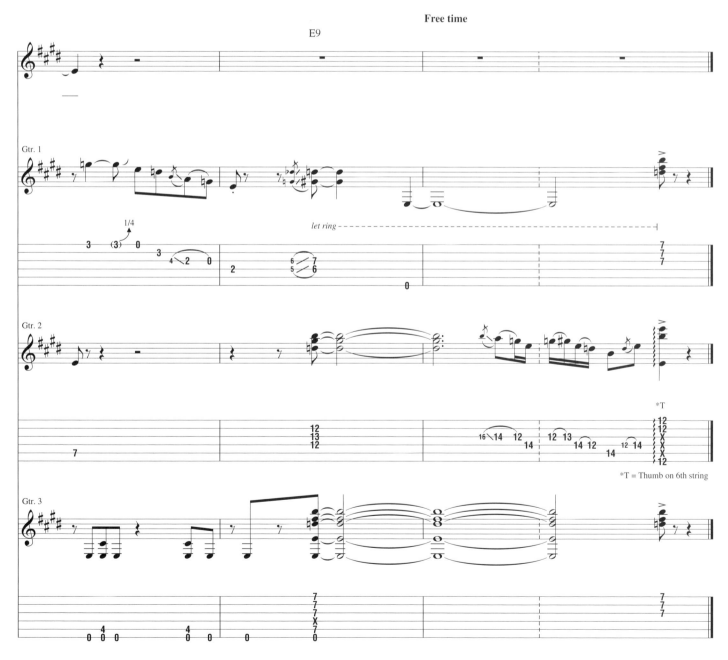

from Tinsley Ellis - *Storm Warning*

To the Devil for a Dime

Words and Music by Chris Long

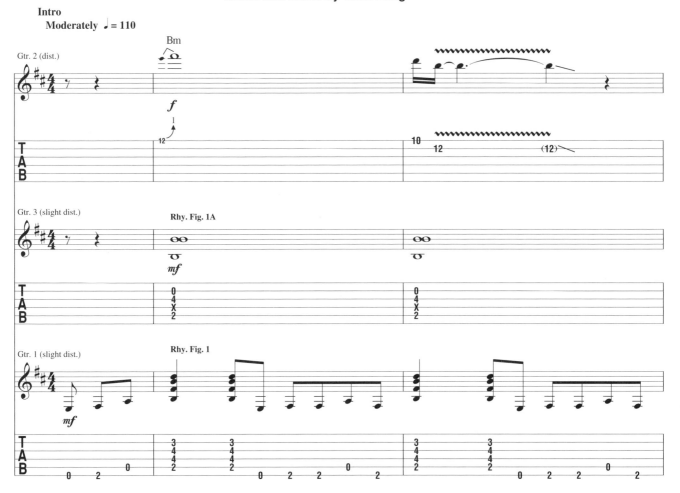

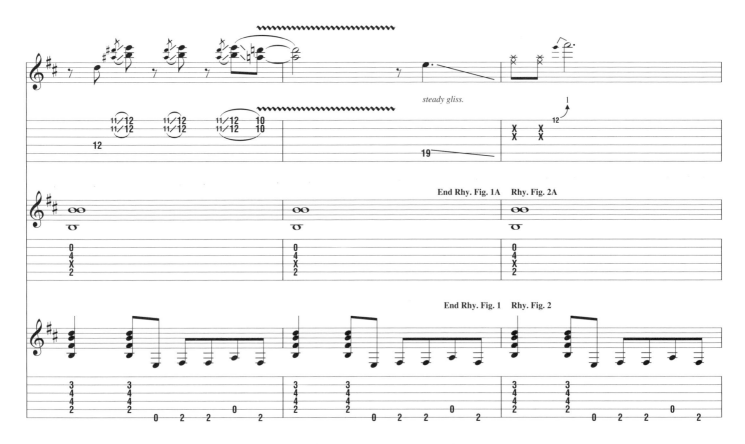

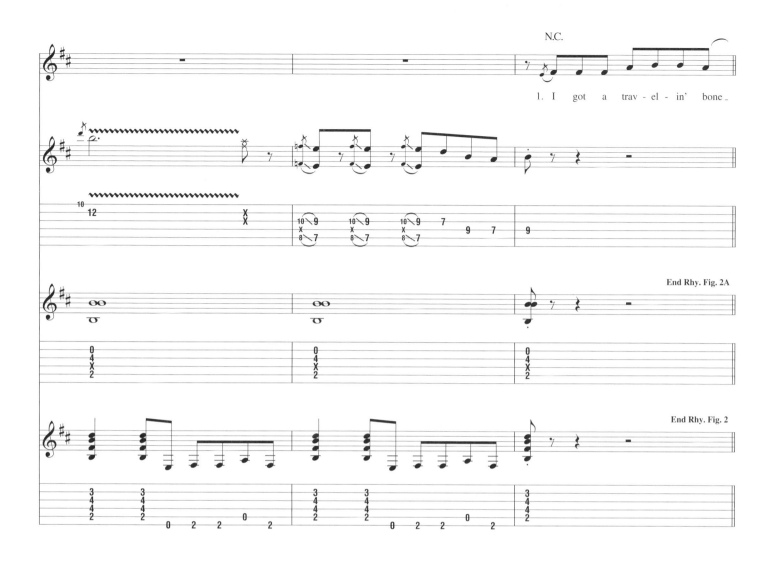

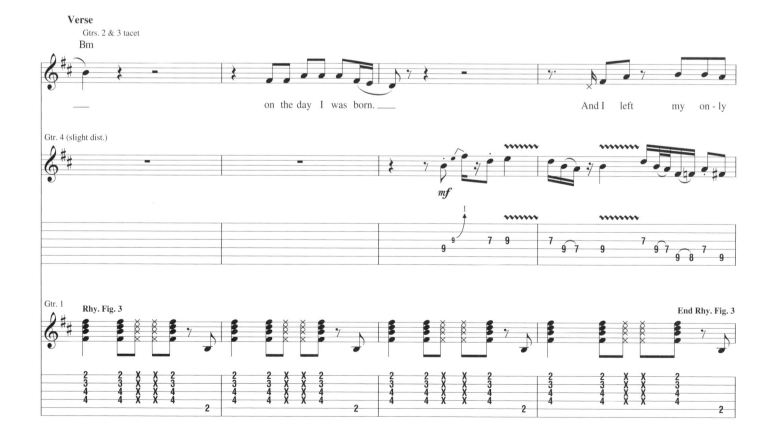

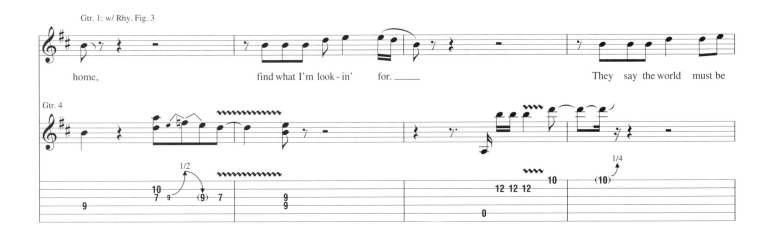

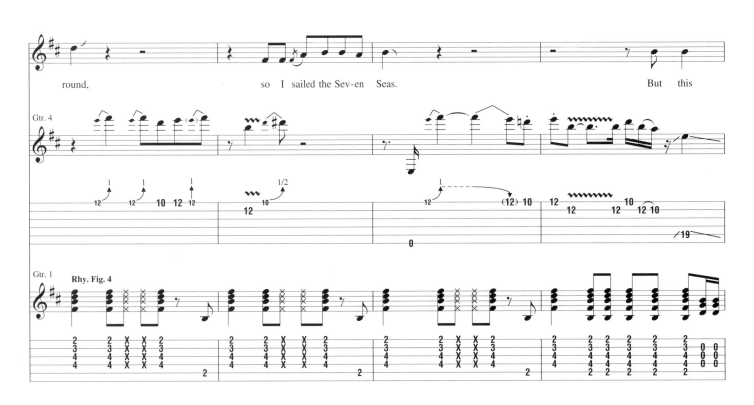

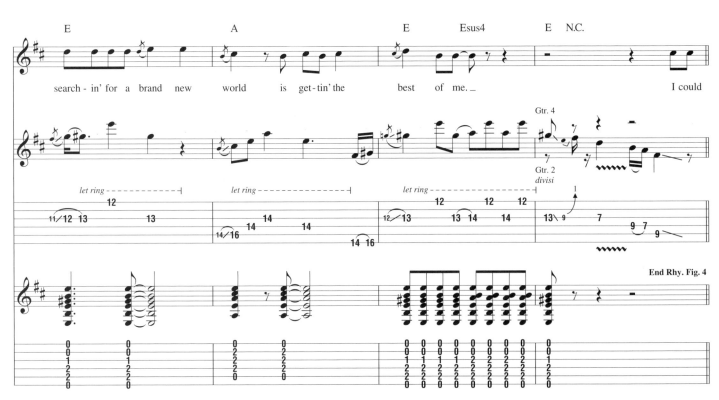

Chorus

Gtrs. 1 & 3: w/ Rhy. Figs. 1 & 1A
Gtr. 2 tacet

Bm

sell my soul ___ to the dev-il for a dime.

(Sell my soul ____ to the dev-il for a dime.)

*Voc. Fig. 1

End Voc. Fig. 1

I could

Gtr. 4

*Refers to downstemmed voc. only.

Gtrs. 1 & 3: w/ Rhy. Figs. 2 & 2A

N.C.

sell my soul ___ to the dev-il for a dime. ___

Sell my soul _____ to the dev-il.)

2. I worked me twen-ty five

Verse

Gtr. 1: w/ Rhy. Fig. 3 (2 times)
Gtr. 4 tacet

Bm

years on that as-sem-bl-y line _____ un-til they fi-n'ly made the

Gtr. 2

P.M. P.M. P.M.

sell my soul __ to the dev-il for a dime. __

Guitar Solo

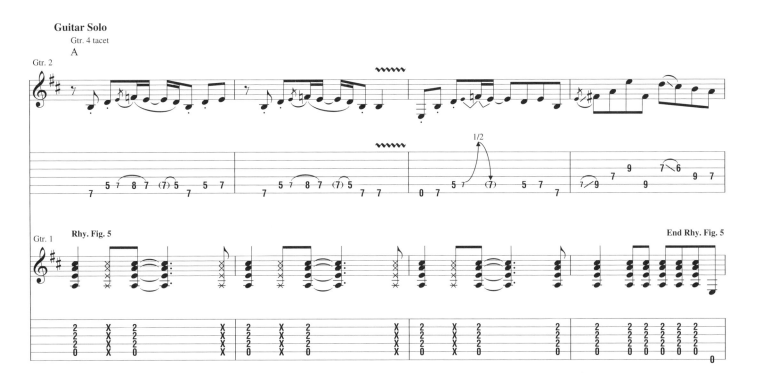

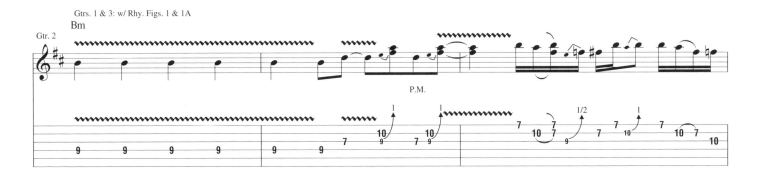

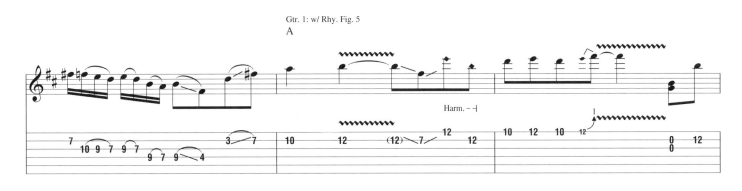

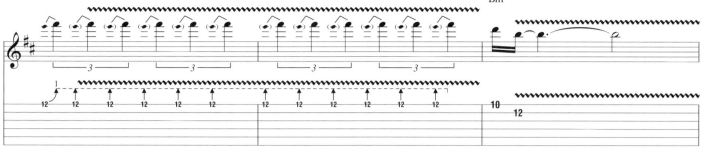

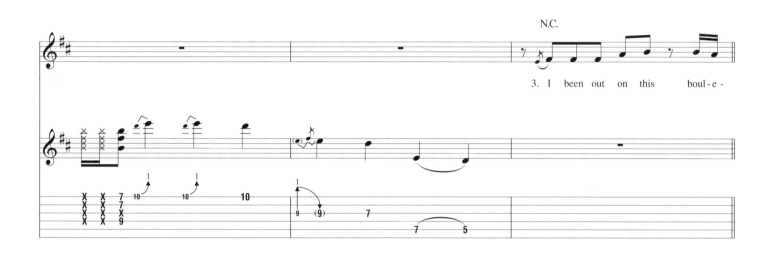

N.C.

3. I been out on this boul-e-

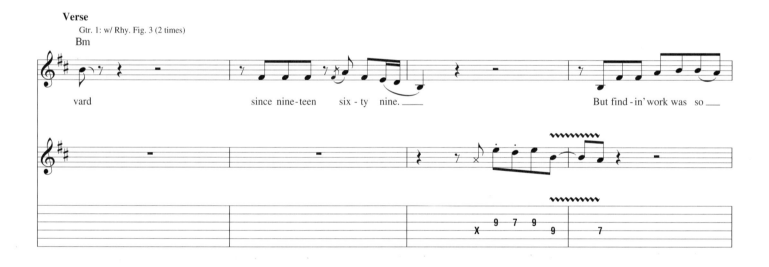

Verse

Gtr. 1: w/ Rhy. Fig. 3 (2 times)

Bm

vard since nine-teen six-ty nine. But find-in' work was so

hard, thought a-bout step-pin' o - ver the line. And now I know some-day my

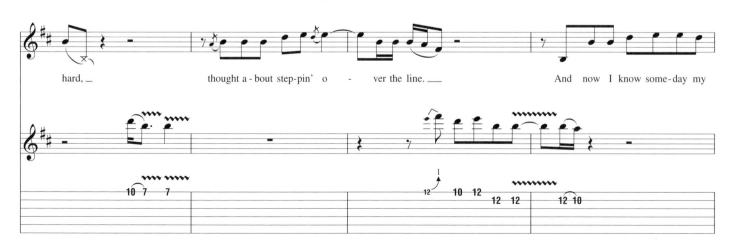

tick-et, my tick-et num-ber got to win. But a

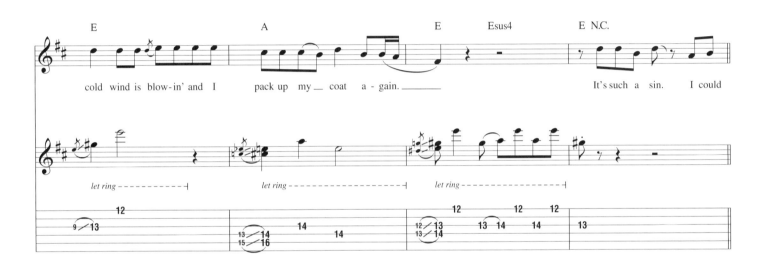

cold wind is blow-in' and I pack up my coat a-gain. It's such a sin. I could

Chorus

Gtrs. 1 & 3: w/ Rhy. Figs. 1 & 1A (2 times)
Gtr. 2 tacet

Bkgd. Voc.: w/ Voc. Fig. 1

sell my soul to the dev-il for a dime. I could

sell my soul___ to the dev-il for a dime.___

Outro-Guitar Solo

Gtr. 1: w/ Rhy. Fig. 5
Gtr. 4 tacet

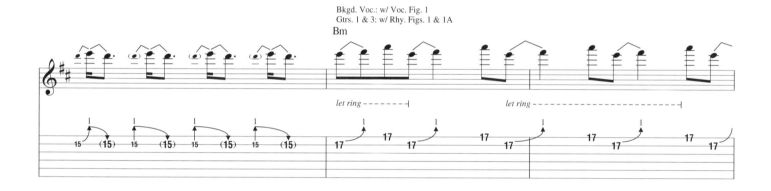

Gtr. 1: w/ Rhy. Fig. 5

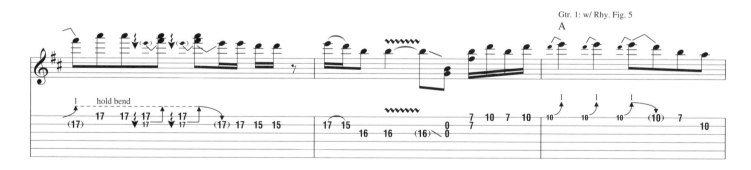

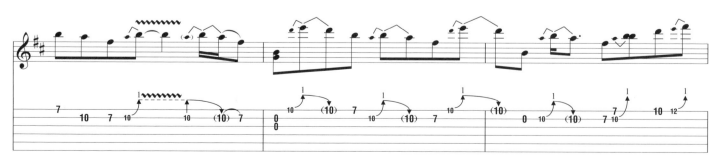

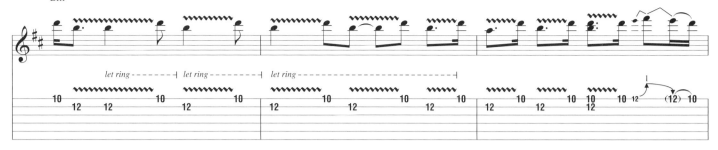

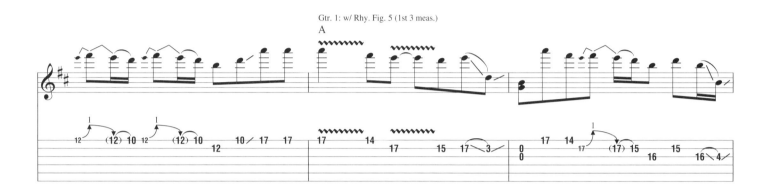

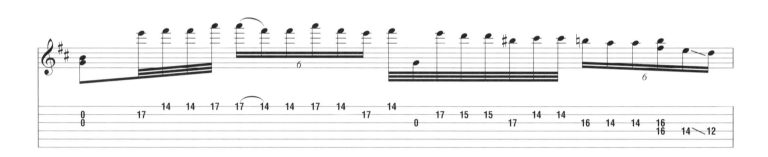

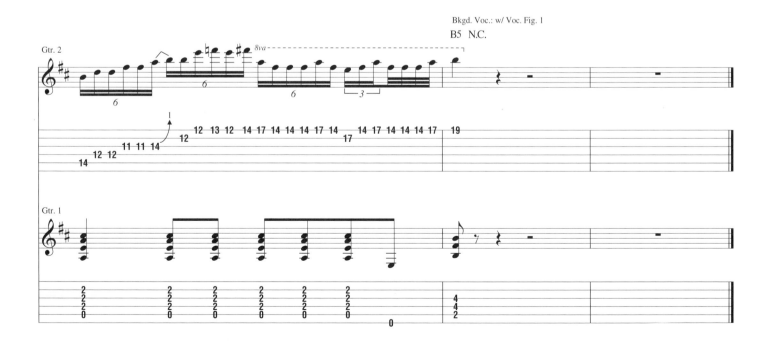

from Lonnie Brooks - *Bayou Lightning*

Voodoo Daddy

Words and Music by Lee Baker Jr.

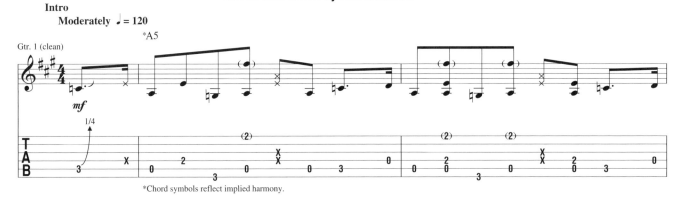

*Chord symbols reflect implied harmony.

mess-in' with __ his daugh - ter, he's gon-na put a spell on me. ____

Verse

Gtr. 2: w/ Rhy. Fig. 1

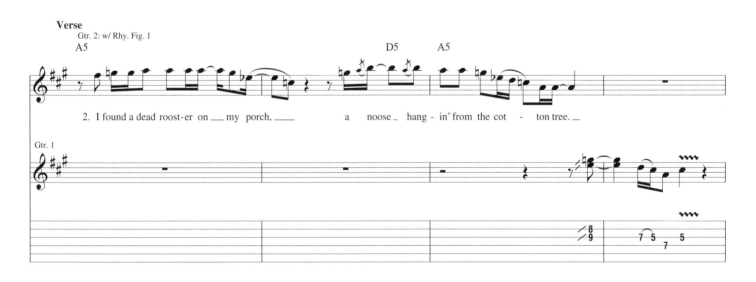

2. I found a dead roost-er on __ my porch, ____ a noose __ hang-in' from the cot - ton tree. __

Gtr. 1

Big black snake __ in my __ bed. ____ Who would, just where I ____ lay ____ my head? __ If I keep

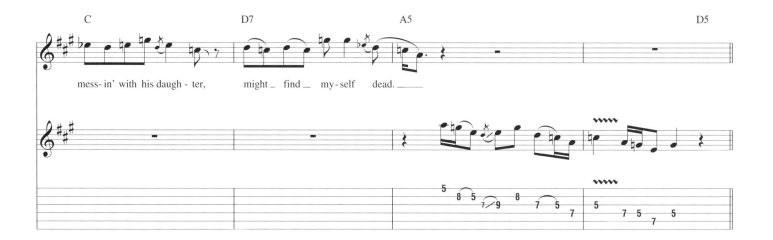

mess-in' with his daugh - ter,   might __ find __ my-self   dead. ____

Guitar Solo
Gtr. 2: w/ Rhy. Fig. 1 (2 times)

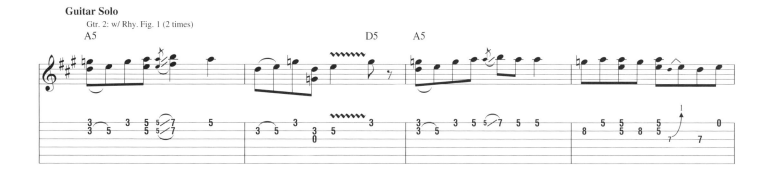

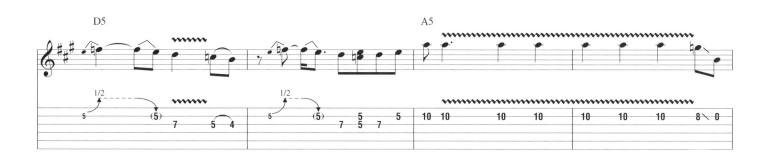

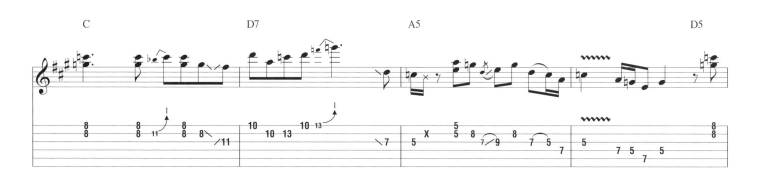

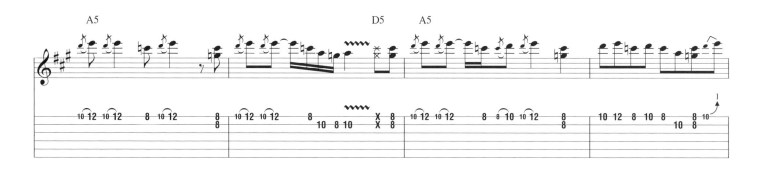

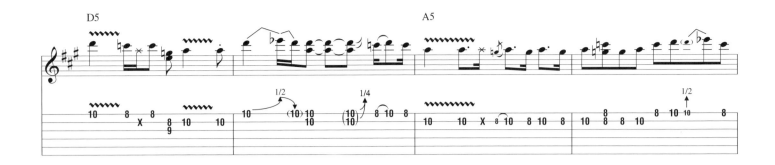

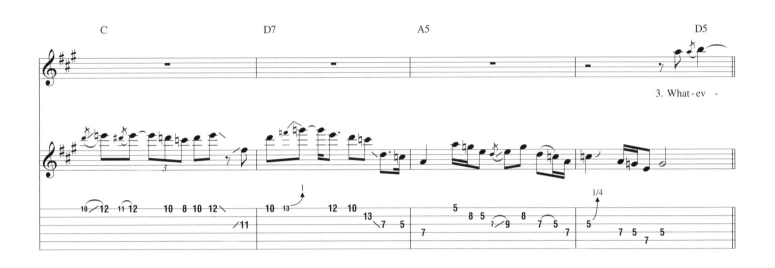

3. What - ev -

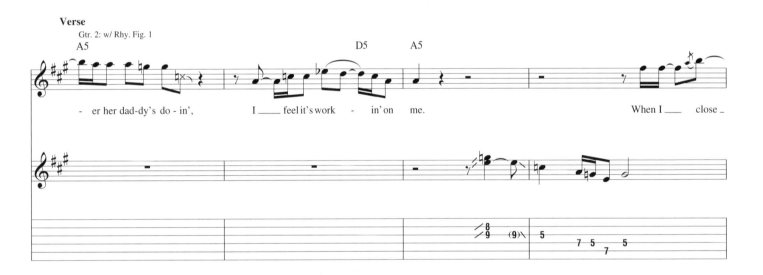

Verse
Gtr. 2: w/ Rhy. Fig. 1

- er her dad-dy's do - in',   I ___ feel it's work - in' on me.   When I ___ close _

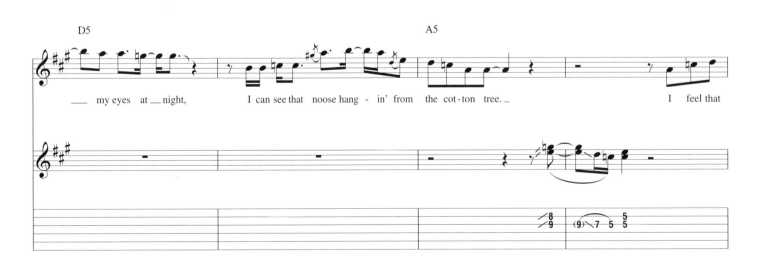

___ my eyes at ___ night,   I can see that noose hang - in' from the cot - ton tree. ___   I feel that

fire in my eye.   His voo - doo is work-in' on me. _____   Oh, __ ba - by!

Guitar Solo
Gtr. 2: w/ Rhy. Fig. 1 (1st 8 meas.)

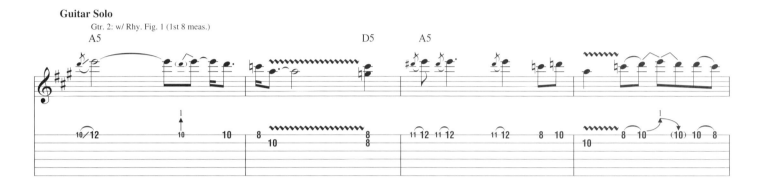

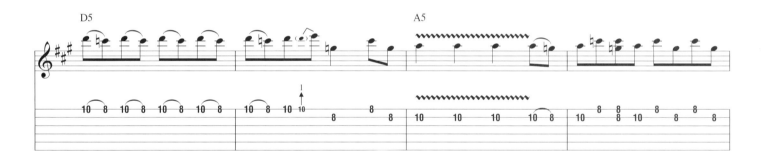

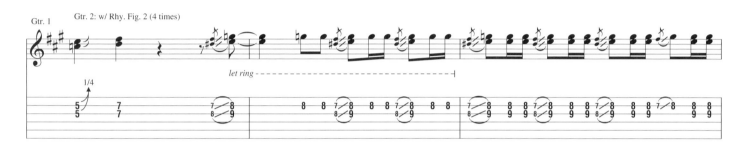

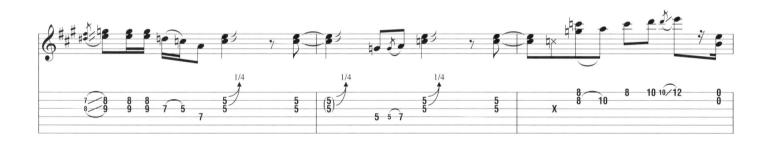

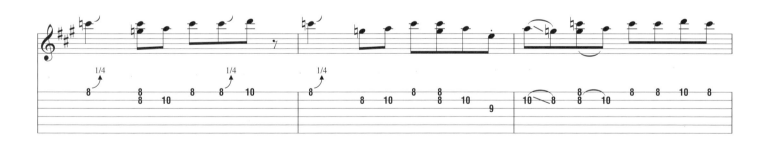

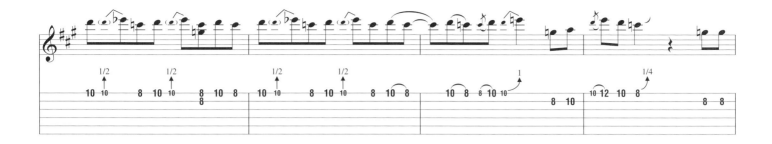

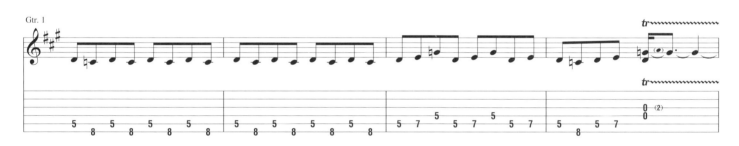

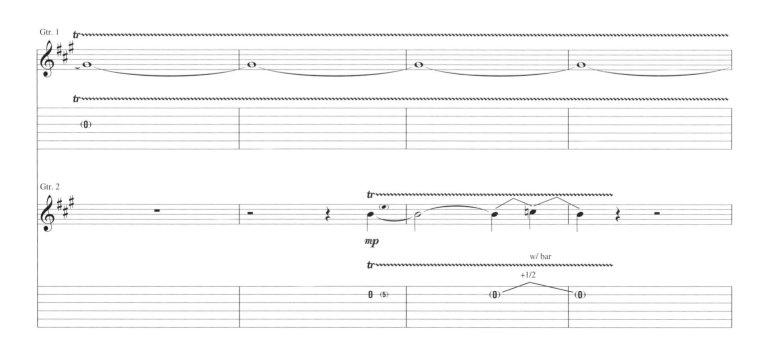

Outro

Spoken: Man, oh, man. Look, her daddy was rough, Jack. He's one of them cats, he's one of them cats from down in

New Orleans. He work that, what you call, voodoo, man. He studied witchcraft, all that

kind of stuff. And look, he put a, a big, black snake in my bed.

He put that... Who put this where I lay my head? He e-ven put a dead roost-

-er on my porch. He e-ven had a noose hang-in' from the cot-ton tree.

I don't care, I don't care, oo, what he do. I'm gon-na

(Hey!)

get there, ha. Oh, ba-by. Come on, now.

Ah, ah, ah, ah.

from Gary Moore - *Bad for You Baby*

Walking Through the Park

Written by Muddy Waters

*Chord symbols reflect overall harmony.

walk for so long, ___ 'til she won't know ___ what to do. Yeah!

Guitar Solo

Uh. ___

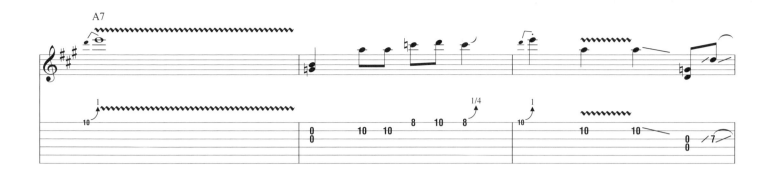

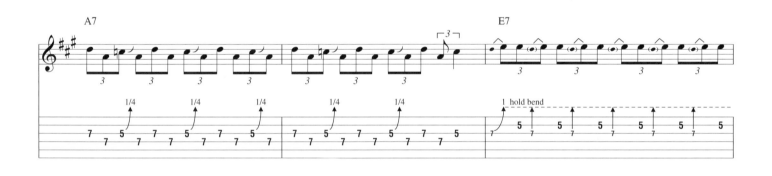

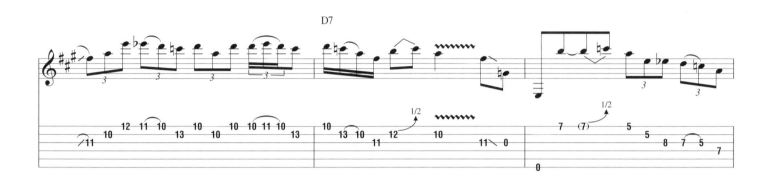

3. I'm __ go -

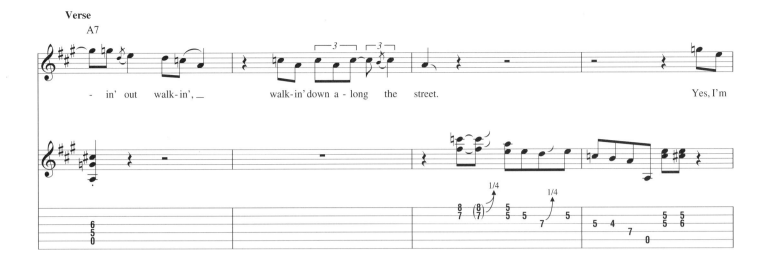

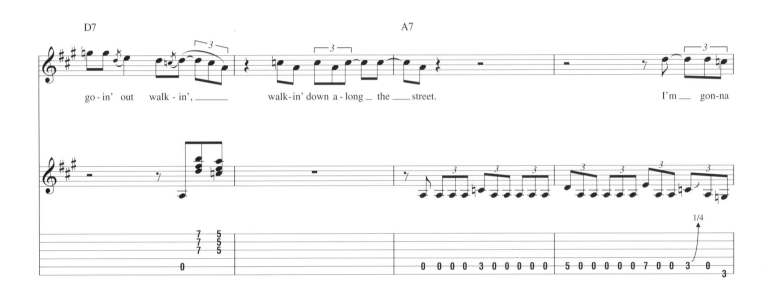

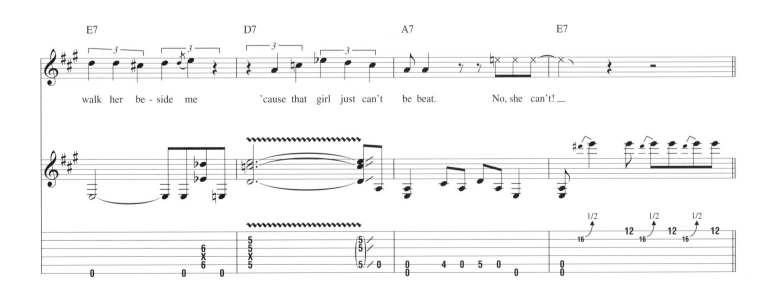

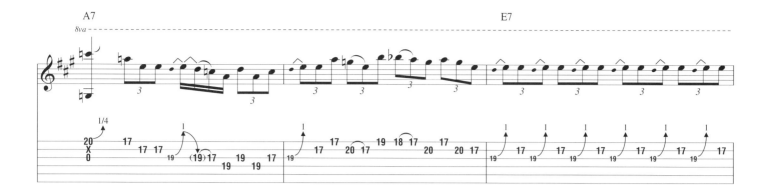

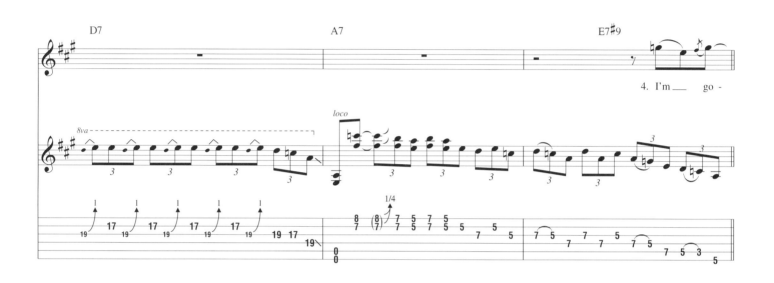

park. ___

I'm ___ gon-na walk in the moon-light

'til the night gets dark.

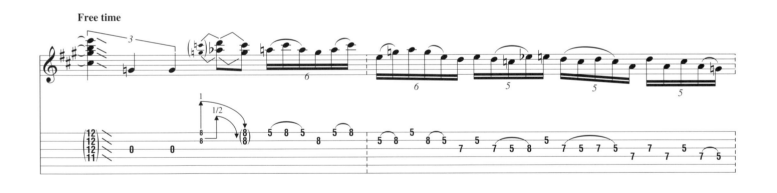

Free time

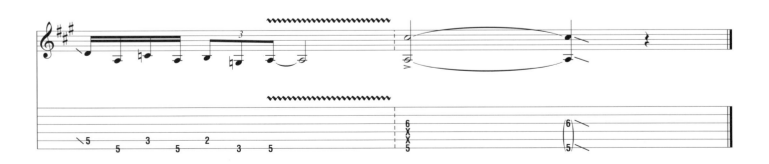

from Albert Cummings - *Working Man*

Workin' Man Blues

Words and Music by Merle Haggard

Tune down 1/2 step:
(low to high) E♭-A♭-D♭-G♭-B♭-E♭

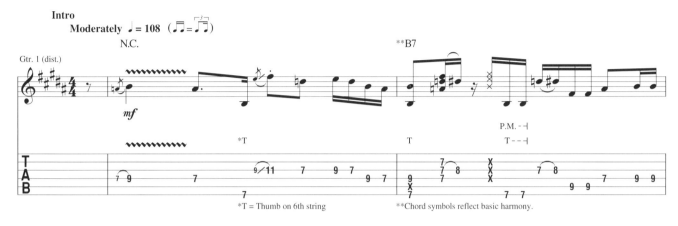

*T = Thumb on 6th string   **Chord symbols reflect basic harmony.

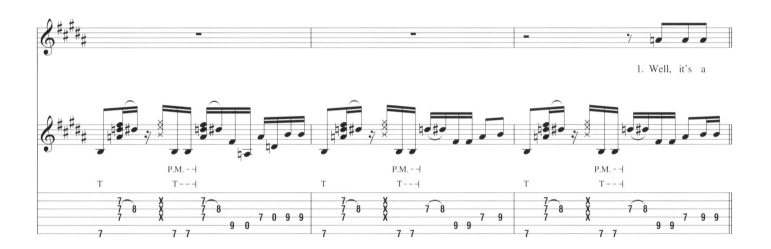

1. Well, it's a

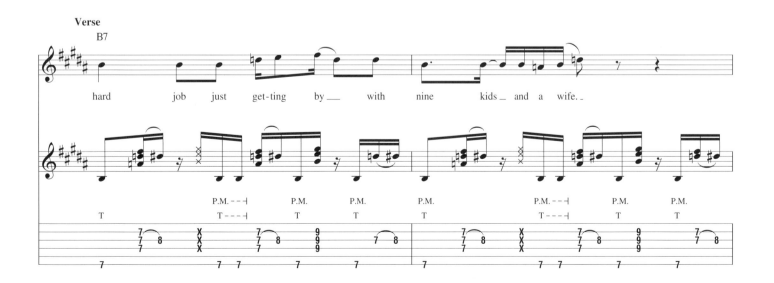

hard   job   just   get-ting   by ___   with   nine   kids ___   and   a   wife. __

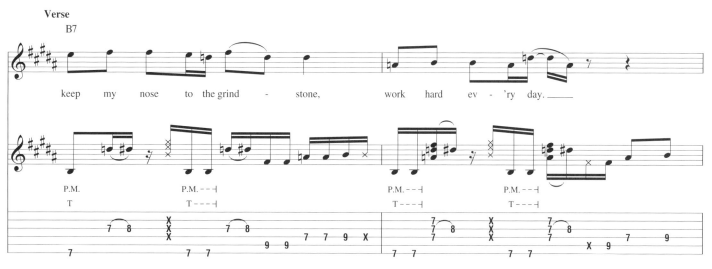

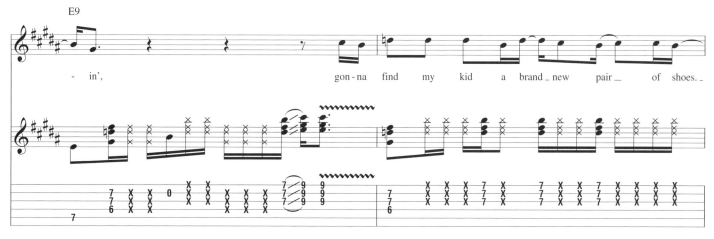

Spoken: Yeah, that's what I'm talk - in' 'bout.

Guitar Solo

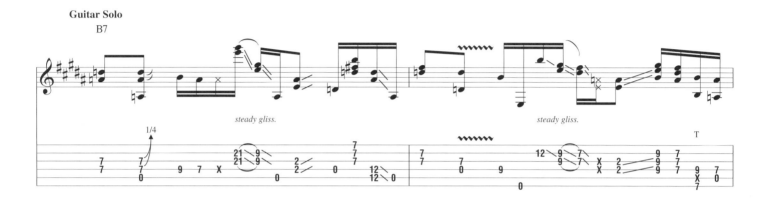

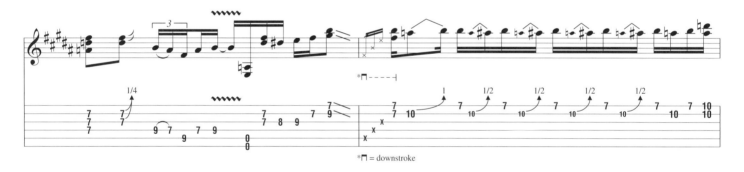

*◻ = downstroke

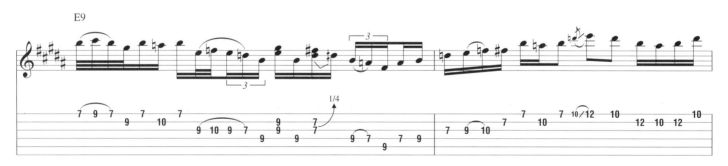

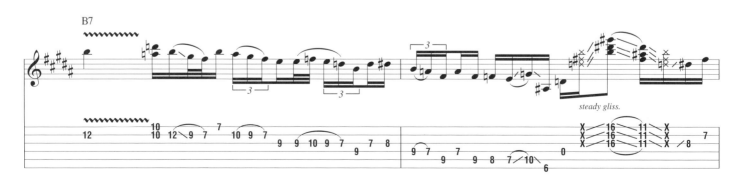

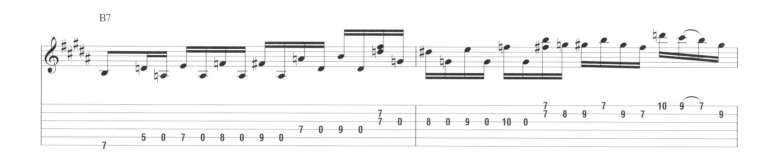

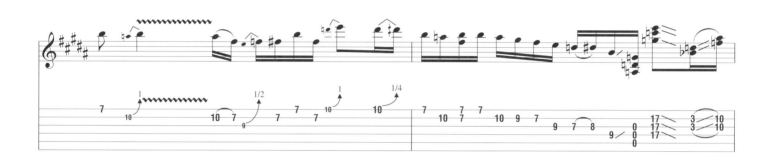

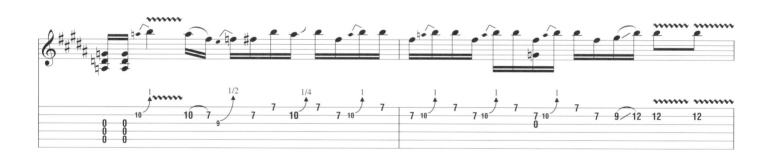

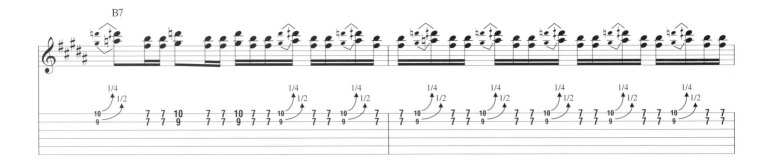

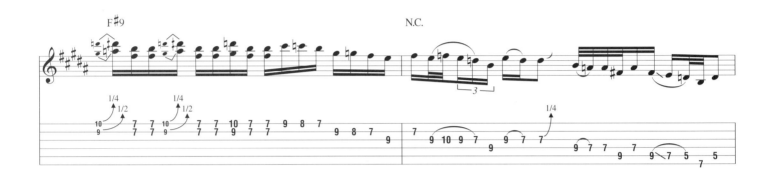

Verse

4. Hey, hey, work-in' man, work-in' man like me.

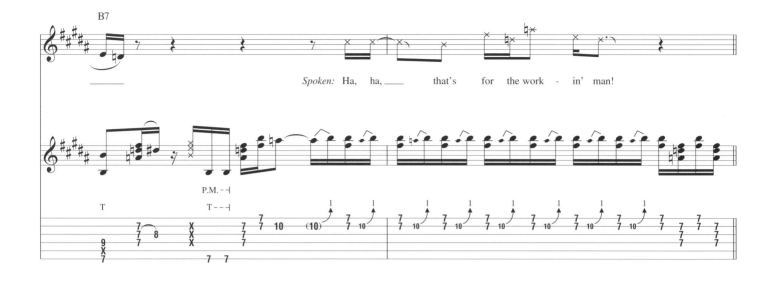

Spoken: Ha, ha, _____ that's for the work - in' man!

Guitar Solo

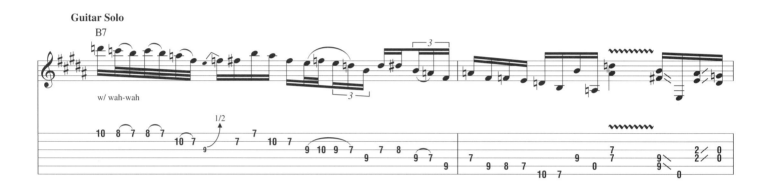

w/ wah-wah

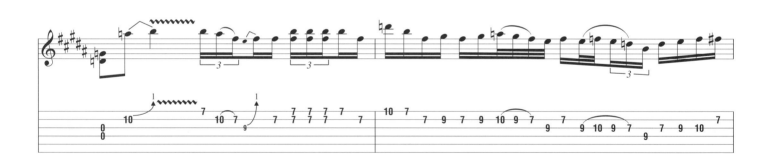

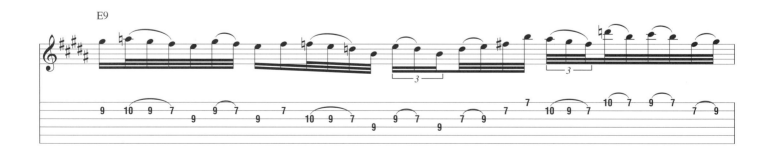

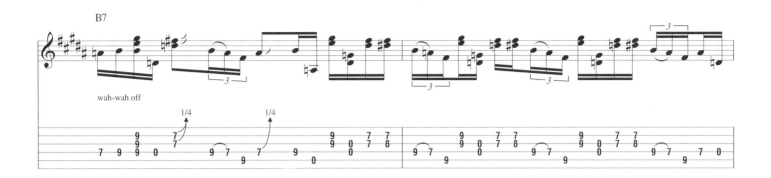

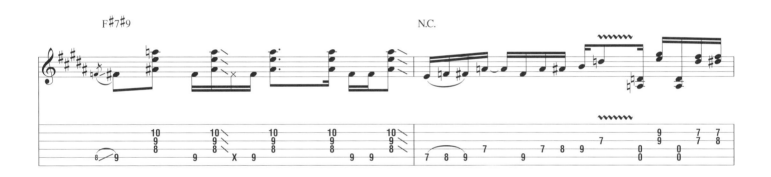

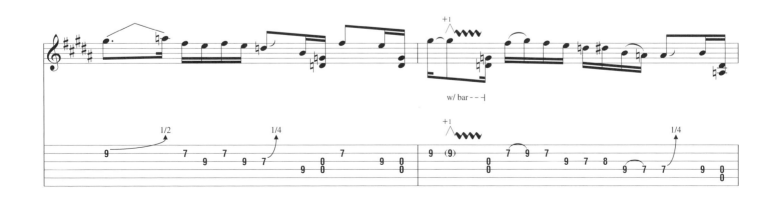

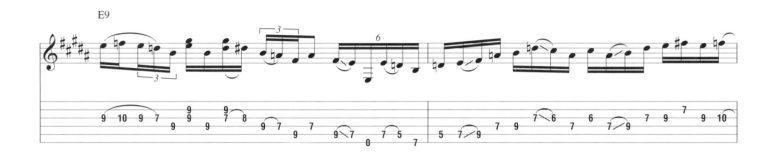

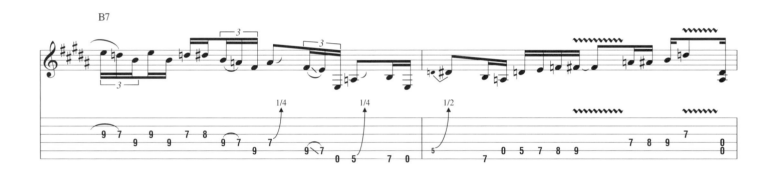

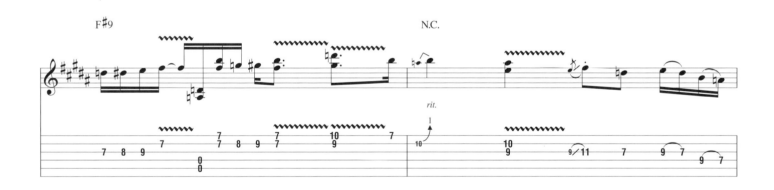

Free time

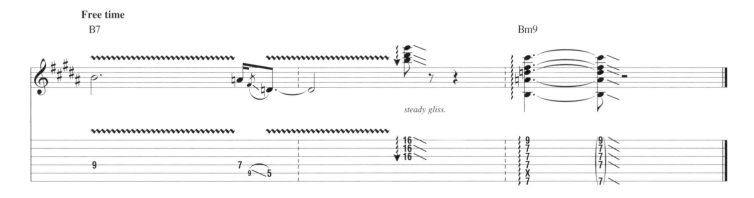

You Give Me Nothing But the Blues

Words and Music by William Longmire

*Chord symbols reflect overall harmony.

**Played behind the beat.

*As before

nights so mis-'ra-ble, you make my days so blue. You give me

noth- in' but the blues, ba - by. I still go for you. Oh,

Guitar Solo

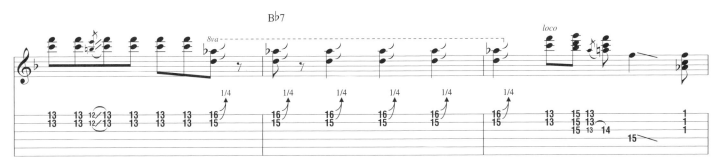

right here!

*Played as even eighth-notes.

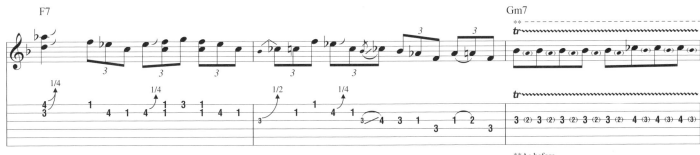

**As before

261

GUITAR NOTATION LEGEND

Guitar music can be notated three different ways: on a *musical staff*, in *tablature*, and in *rhythm slashes*.

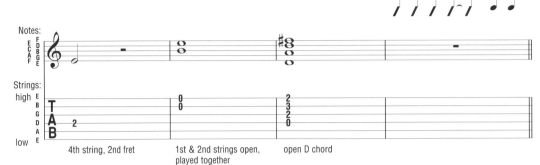

RHYTHM SLASHES are written above the staff. Strum chords in the rhythm indicated. Use the chord diagrams found at the top of the first page of the transcription for the appropriate chord voicings. Round noteheads indicate single notes.

THE MUSICAL STAFF shows pitches and rhythms and is divided by bar lines into measures. Pitches are named after the first seven letters of the alphabet.

TABLATURE graphically represents the guitar fingerboard. Each horizontal line represents a string, and each number represents a fret.

4th string, 2nd fret · 1st & 2nd strings open, played together · open D chord

---

HALF-STEP BEND: Strike the note and bend up 1/2 step.

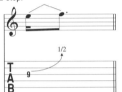

WHOLE-STEP BEND: Strike the note and bend up one step.

GRACE NOTE BEND: Strike the note and immediately bend up as indicated.

SLIGHT (MICROTONE) BEND: Strike the note and bend up 1/4 step.

BEND AND RELEASE: Strike the note and bend up as indicated, then release back to the original note. Only the first note is struck.

PRE-BEND: Bend the note as indicated, then strike it.

VIBRATO: The string is vibrated by rapidly bending and releasing the note with the fretting hand.

WIDE VIBRATO: The pitch is varied to a greater degree by vibrating with the fretting hand.

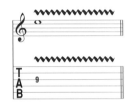

HAMMER-ON: Strike the first (lower) note with one finger, then sound the higher note (on the same string) with another finger by fretting it without picking.

PULL-OFF: Place both fingers on the notes to be sounded. Strike the first note and without picking, pull the finger off to sound the second (lower) note.

LEGATO SLIDE: Strike the first note and then slide the same fret-hand finger up or down to the second note. The second note is not struck.

SHIFT SLIDE: Same as legato slide, except the second note is struck.

TRILL: Very rapidly alternate between the notes indicated by continuously hammering on and pulling off.

TAPPING: Hammer ("tap") the fret indicated with the pick-hand index or middle finger and pull off to the note fretted by the fret hand.

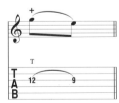

NATURAL HARMONIC: Strike the note while the fret-hand lightly touches the string directly over the fret indicated.

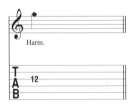

PINCH HARMONIC: The note is fretted normally and a harmonic is produced by adding the edge of the thumb or the tip of the index finger of the pick hand to the normal pick attack.

PICK SCRAPE: The edge of the pick is rubbed down (or up) the string, producing a scratchy sound.

MUFFLED STRINGS: A percussive sound is produced by laying the fret hand across the string(s) without depressing, and striking them with the pick hand.

PALM MUTING: The note is partially muted by the pick hand lightly touching the string(s) just before the bridge.

RAKE: Drag the pick across the strings indicated with a single motion.

TREMOLO PICKING: The note is picked as rapidly and continuously as possible.

VIBRATO BAR DIVE AND RETURN: The pitch of the note or chord is dropped a specified number of steps (in rhythm), then returned to the original pitch.

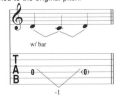

VIBRATO BAR SCOOP: Depress the bar just before striking the note, then quickly release the bar.

VIBRATO BAR DIP: Strike the note and then immediately drop a specified number of steps, then release back to the original pitch.